CW00408164

Charlie

Charlie
An Autobiography

Charlie Nicholas
with Ken Gallacher

Stanley Paul
London Melbourne Auckland Johannesburg

First published in 1986 by Stanley Paul & Co. Ltd,
Brookmount House, 62–65 Chandos Place, Covent Garden,
London WC2N 4NW

Stanley Paul is an imprint of the Century Hutchinson Publishing
Group

Century Hutchinson Publishing Group (Australia) Pty Ltd
16–22 Church Street, Hawthorn, Melbourne, Victoria 3122

Century Hutchinson Group (NZ) Ltd
32–34 View Road, PO Box 40–086, Glenfield, Auckland 10

Century Hutchinson Group (SA) Pty Ltd
PO Box 337, Bergvlei 2012, South Africa

Phototypeset in Linotron Baskerville by
Input Typesetting Ltd, London SW19 8DR

Printed and bound in Great Britain by
Anchor Brendon Ltd, Tiptree, Essex

British Library Cataloguing in Publication Data

Nicholas, Charlie
    Charlie : an autobiography.
    1. Nicholas, Charlie   2. Soccer players
    —Scotland—Biography
    I. Title   II. Gallacher, Ken
    796.334'092'4   GV942.7.N/

ISBN 0 09 163820 8

Contents

Dedication

To Mum and Dad
with thanks for all the encouragement and
sacrifices that made everything possible

Acknowledgements

I'd like to place on record my grateful thanks to the following people for all their help, encouragement and support: Jock Stein, Billy McNeill, Danny McGrain, Frank Cairney, Frank Connor, Jerome Anderson, the Mitchell family, Jimmy Steel and Kenny Dalglish.

Photograph Acknowledgements

Thanks are due to the following for allowing the use of copyright photographs: Associated Sports Photography, Colorsport, Sportapics, and the *Sunday Mirror*.

1

Early Days

I was about twelve years old when I came to the conclusion that nothing came easy in life. Until then everything had seemed OK. A good family life. Good mates to play football with in the Wyndford housing scheme in Glasgow's Maryhill. And a teacher at the school who turned a blind eye when I missed classes because he thought I'd make it as a footballer.

Then my Dad was made redundant. On the dole he was, and I needed a new pair of football boots. For the first time in my life he knocked me back for something that I thought was important, something that I knew he also believed was important to me. So I was left playing football in my gym shoes – or 'gutties' as they are known in Glasgow. When he was back in work I got the boots but that lesson stayed with me.

Now people look at me and say I get it easy. Playing for Arsenal, being photographed on the London nightclub scene, and with as many pairs of boots as I want. I've boots for training, boots for playing on one surface and boots for playing on another. If I want another pair I only have to lift the telephone and they'll be delivered to Highbury. But none of them will ever mean as much to me as the pair of boots my Dad gave me when he got a job again.

There were no sponsors around to give me handouts then. There was no one from Nike to provide the style of boots I wanted or the trendiest tracksuits. There was only my Dad and the rest of the family, and I know how much it hurt him back then when he had to say no to a new pair of boots.

No one has ever encouraged me as much as my Dad did. There were others who helped when my career got under way, but in the beginning there was Dad and me and the streets of Glasgow where so many other players learned the skills of football.

When I was only four or five years old I wanted to make football my career, and that's all down to my old man. Every morning when I woke there was a ball at the side of my bed and my Dad was always ready to kick it about with me. He was football mad. It's the way he was brought up and it's the way that he brought me up. He went to see the Celtic every week then and took me with him to the terracing.

But, more important, he came out whenever he could to kick the ball around with me in the street. There must have been times when he said to himself, 'What am I doing here, playing with a young lad?' But then I didn't think that; all I knew was the importance of kicking that ball about. If your old man was out there doing it with you, then it had to be something special. It must have meant a lot to him, and because of that the game took on a real importance for me.

It was a strange situation. There was I, aged five, asking my Dad if he wanted to come out to play, and there was he doing it. Everyone in that housing scheme played football then, but he was the only old man who joined in all the games. He must have had a dream that I would play professionally one day, although he never said as much. Yet always, for as long as I can remember, I knew that this was where he wanted me to succeed. And if success came in the form of me playing for his beloved Celtic, then it was going to be all the better for him.

The area where we played was called the playpen. All the lads in the housing scheme used to be there from first thing in the morning to last thing at night in the school holidays, just playing football. That was all we did, and it was all we wanted to do. Most of my mates were a few years older than I was, and my next-door neighbour was Jim Duffy, who plays for Dundee now. We were at Celtic together. Duff was just one of the good players who took part in those games, but a lot of the other lads didn't get the chance to go professional as we did. We had some games back then!

All we did was play football. We were in that playpen for hour after hour, and yet we loved every minute of it. All the skills I have were developed then – moving around in a restricted area, controlling the ball quickly as it broke to you off the concrete, avoiding tackles when you were caught in a corner: all the street tricks which you could refine and use later in life when you found yourself on a real pitch in a real game as a member of a real team. And, if you were lucky, playing on grass instead of the ash pitches which Glasgow was infamous for!

At that time, too, the game was more fun. No one tried to organize it too much. You got up in the morning, pulled on your gutties and went out to play. You didn't ask what position you would be playing or anything like that. You just played. You didn't worry about the kit you wore, like the kids seem to do nowadays. You couldn't worry about it because you didn't have it. You had your sandshoes and that was your lot.

School was an interruption, something which intruded into the time that should have been spent playing football. I went to St Columba of Iona, but I hated school. My mates were OK, and getting a game of football on a Saturday for the school team was great. I enjoyed PE, except for odd occasions in the winter when we had to go into the gym and dance with the birds! But lessons were a problem. I spent most of the time trying to work out how to duck classes without being caught. I usually managed to sneak away, but when it came to the maths classes the teacher, Peter Sullivan, used to hunt me down. He didn't think that I was cut out to be another Einstein, but he was a football man and wanted me to stay out of trouble so I could play in the school team on a Saturday morning. He saw some potential in me then. That was when I was about twelve. He was a hard teacher and although I couldn't dodge his classes he gave me an easy time. He'd get me to take messages to other teachers and things like that because he knew that I wasn't interested in learning.

He was a Celtic man and I used to see him when I was at Celtic and have seen him several times since. Sometimes, when I'm outside Hampden, I'll hear a shout of 'Nicholas!', and I know that it's Peter. It's never 'Charlie!', always 'Nicholas!', just the way it was at school. I always know straightaway whenever I hear that shout that my old teacher's going to be watching me. He was a big help to me when I was at school.

The next guy to guide me and really launch me in my senior career was Frank Cairney, who runs the Celtic Boys' Club. People looking at my career see that I played with Celtic Boys' Club, then made the transition to the Celtic ground staff, then went into the reserves and finally into the first team. It looks so easy and yet it was not like that at all. There was a spell when I wanted nothing more than to leave the Boys' Club and go and play somewhere else. Frank Cairney was the man who rescued me.

When I was about fourteen I went through a terrible time at Celtic Boys' Club. I hardly ever got a game. That went on for a whole year, and even when I turned fifteen I was still struggling. At twelve and thirteen I'd been picking up loads of awards as player of the year and so on with the Boys' Club. Now I was a couple of years older and I couldn't get a game. I panicked. I used to say to myself, 'What am I going to do? I'll have to get a job.' I couldn't think of anything that I wanted to do other than play football. It was a real crisis for me. At that age you worry about things because you can't always understand what is happening to you and why.

The reason was that the lad who ran the younger

team, a fellow called Bobby Crilley, insisted on playing me on the right wing. And there was a natural outside right called Tommy Coakley, a little lad from Motherwell, who was keeping me out. Bobby Crilley appeared to have a different view of things from the lads I had played with up to then. It was a strange time for me . . . and for my Dad. If I hadn't still been playing in the school team on a Saturday morning, I don't know what I would have done. I was scoring up to six or seven goals in a game on a Saturday morning and then not getting a game for the club on the Sunday. Or if I did get a game I'd be standing shivering on the right wing waiting for the ball to come to me. Luckily clubs who watched me in the school team let Peter Sullivan know they were interested in me. Ipswich and Wolves and Manchester City all asked me down to train with them.

I actually started out playing for Rangers Boys' Club because I could get a game there. Then my Uncle Tommy – he's dead now – managed to get me a trial with the Celtic club. That's what my Dad and I wanted, but on the day we went up to see about the trial there were thirty or forty lads and I was about fifth last in the line-up. At that time I was playing at inside right, but before I got to the front of the queue at least ten other boys said that they played inside right. So I said I was an inside left, even though, at that time, my left foot was nothing to write home about. I've always been lucky enough to have two good feet, but I hadn't worried too much about my left foot until then. That was when I was ten, and all the awards I won in the next few years came as an inside left.

Then I was turned into a right winger, which baffled me. I'm not the paciest player in the game. I'm quick and sharp over maybe ten yards or a little more, which can be deceptive, but at that age I didn't have the sharpness. I was simply relying on skill. Yet I was being asked to knock the ball past defenders and run. I could beat the defender any number of times but I couldn't run. It wasn't the way I played the game.

So for two years I was in and out of the Boys' Club team, and out much more than in. At the end of the second season of misery – and it was misery for me – my Dad suggested that I should leave the club and go and play for someone else. He didn't want me playing for anyone else. I didn't want to play for anyone else. But he was advising me to do what he thought would be best for me in the long run so far as a football career was concerned. He was right to say it.

But I decided to hang on until the start of the next season when I was due to step up to the Under-16 side. That's when I came under Frank Cairney's wing. He watched me in training and put me in the team as a sweeper. It didn't worry me at all. Big Frank was giving me a game every week and just to be playing for the club again on a regular basis was good enough for me.

I played in that position for a spell and had a great time. I went down to Ipswich as a sweeper and Bobby Robson, who was manager at Portman Road then, wanted to sign me. I honestly thought about signing for them because it was so good down there. The one thing that held me back was the fact that they played in blue, the same colour as Rangers. There was no way I could play in blue. My old man would have never come to watch me if I'd played in blue!

Frank Cairney was of massive importance to me at that time and I'll never forget what he did for me. When I came back from Ipswich he went to see Jock Stein, who was the Celtic manager then, and his assistant Dave McParland. Frank pointed out that Bobby Robson wanted to sign me, that Wolves were interested, and that if they wanted me for Celtic they would have to move quickly. Jock was fairly keen because he'd seen me playing a few times. But Dave McParland didn't care whether I signed or not. He didn't think I could play. Frank persuaded Jock to sign me. It was really because of Frank that I signed for Celtic. In fact, he reminds me very much of Jock Stein. He's the kind of man who always sets you targets and coaxes the best out of you all the time.

Eventually he moved me out of the sweeper's position. It was only by accident that I had been played there in the first place. Big Frank admitted to me later that he had been hesitant about keeping me on with the Boys' Club, as I hadn't played a lot for them in the previous two years. So when I stepped up to his team he toyed with the idea of telling me I'd be better off elsewhere. But he must have seen something in me and so he kept me on after the initial pre-season training. I dropped into defence in one of the practice games and he saw straightaway that I could read the game well and could pass the ball, so he left me there. It took him about a month to realize that I couldn't stay there. He came to me one day and said, 'Your talent is being hindered by playing back there. I'll have to move you up front.' I'd waited more than two years to hear someone with the club tell me that! Frank was the first of the officials to see where my real position was. Once Frank moved me up front I never looked back.

It had been a terrible time for me. Heart-breaking. And for my Dad as well. He has always hurt along with me. When I was playing at Celtic he'd be there, and if I had a bad game and someone started going on about my not playing well he'd be snapping at them because he was feeling what I was feeling. When I went back to play for Arsenal at Celtic Park in a pre-season game some of the crowd booed me. That really got to the old man. I don't think he has been back to Parkhead since that day. He usually goes to watch my young brother with the Boys' Club.

Being booed upset me too, because I've been a Celtic man ever since my Dad took me to the terraces as a youngster. I thought that the fans knew that. Most of them do, I guess. It took me a little while to get over it and I can't forgive the fans who did it. But when I went up to Hampden to see Celtic win the Scottish Cup in the final against Dundee United, the fans I met that day helped me get over being jeered. They were magic. I went home wearing a Celtic scarf that someone had given me. It helped my Dad as well. We were able to forget the other business and just enjoy seeing our team win the Cup.

The great thing was that I could go back, and the love I had for the club returned. No matter what takes place, you can't turn your back on the club that gave you your start. There will always be a place in my heart for Celtic because it was through them that I learned my trade. And through them that I met Frank Cairney, who taught me good habits early on in life. The way he handled me then, the way he guided me when I was an impressionable teenager, has given me the confidence to go on and achieve whatever I have achieved in the game. So much is down to the fact that he picked me up when I was at my lowest and that he convinced Celtic they had to sign me.

I always knew that I had natural ability and I never stopped believing in that ability. But without someone like Frank Cairney my faith in myself might have withered. When I signed for Celtic at fifteen and a half I knew Davie McParland didn't want me there. That knowledge, coming so soon after two years of misery with the Boys' Club, made life a bit of an uphill struggle for me then. But just when it looked as if I would never get the chance to show what I could do I broke into the reserves. Lads like Willie McStay and Danny Crainie and Mark Reid were there already. They were all signed before me. As each one joined the Boys' Club he was signed. I was the one who had to wait for that chance to arrive. I'd been with the Boys' Club for six seasons before Celtic finally signed me up. I was the last of that group.

They are good mates and I stay close to them, because we shared some good days together. When you have been through good times with a bunch of mates there is a bond between you. We still go on holiday together every summer – Willie, who is at Celtic Park still, little

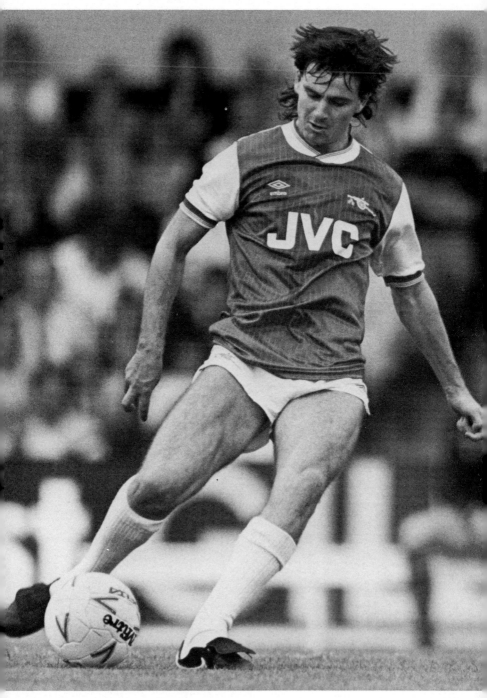

Charlie - showing all the style that the North Bank love

 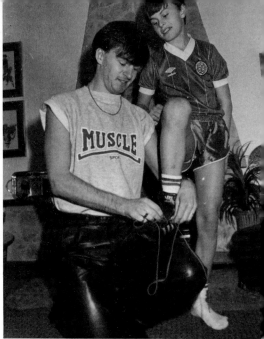

Above left: On holiday with sister Janice – and Charlie has a ball with him. 'The ball was never far away,' his parents point out

Above right: Little brother Stephen may be following in Charlie's footsteps. Already he has been picked for Scotland's schoolboy squad. Here big brother sees to his boots

Below: Happy family – Charlie with his Mum and Dad relaxing at the playground in Maryhill where he kicked off his career

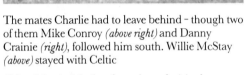

The mates Charlie had to leave behind – though two of them Mike Conroy *(above right)* and Danny Crainie *(right)*, followed him south. Willie McStay *(above)* stayed with Celtic

Below: Murdo MacLeod watches admiringly as Charlie runs rings around Kenny Black, then of Rangers

Celebration time for Charlie as Tommy Burns *(left)* and Frank McGarvey *(right)* congratulate him after scoring the winner in an Old Firm clash

Next door neighbours in Maryhill, Jim Duffy (now with Dundee) and Charlie check the headlines

Danny, who is with Wolves, and Mike Conroy, who joined the group a little bit later, and is now with Blackpool. It's great to get together and see each other again. During the season Danny and Mike come to London to see me or I go up to see them. I would like to go to Charlton to see Mark Reid, who is playing there now. Frank Cairney's influence was partly responsible for our friendship because he used to say, 'Never grow up, stay as you are for as long as you can'. He could see how well we all got on together.

People must have expected me to change when I moved to Arsenal. They would see pictures of me at some nightclub and think I'd become all flash and grown away from my mates. It hasn't happened that way at all and I don't think it ever will.

When Danny McGrain and Kenny Dalglish get together, for example, they are still the same. They kid around just like they used to do when they were in the reserves at Celtic Park. If that pair can do it, it's got to be a good thing!

I don't want to change. I'm determined not to get too carried away with myself. I feel at my most relaxed when I'm with my mates, and I'd rather be sitting in an ordinary pub in Blackpool with Mike Conroy on a Saturday night than in some trendy nightspot in London. It's good for me to see them as often as possible. They haven't made it as big as I have in the game and it helps keep my feet on the ground when I hear about some of their problems. Little Danny has had more than his share with Wolves. There have been weeks there when the wages haven't arrived for the lads. So although I'm with a big club, I can't forget the other side of the game. And I'll never forget where I came from. If I did, then I would be a lesser person.

Anyhow, my Dad would probably disown me. Or, at least, he'd refuse to kick a ball around with me in that playpen in Maryhill!

2

My London Problems

It was Frank Sinatra who used to sing 'Saturday Night Is the Loneliest Night of the Week'. I didn't believe him when I lived in Glasgow. It took the move to London to bring out the meaning of that song because, despite all the stories of my supposedly fabulous lifestyle, I've never spent so many Saturday nights on my own in the house as I have done since moving to Arsenal. The old cliché about London being a lonely place is true at times. And Saturday night, the one night when I can go out without anyone pointing a finger at me – because it's after a game – is the night on which I feel really lonely.

If you go out after having won that afternoon supporters will come up and clap you on the back and say, 'Well done.' Then you can explain that you're with friends and they'll leave you alone. But a Saturday night after a defeat is very different. That's when the fans have a right to ask you what went wrong and you have some kind of duty to try to answer them. You can't walk away from someone who is helping pay your wages. And so a night out can be spoiled because you can't pay attention to the people you are with. It's a problem, and to overcome the problem I have often stayed in the house.

It can be very lonely at times. I have a few really good mates down here in London, and there are also the players, the lads I train with and play with week after week. But most of them are married and it's not so easy to fit in with their way of life. You can't phone up a married lad and ask, 'Are you going down the pub for a pint?' because it might upset his family life. And you can't expect your mates to be there all the time because they have girlfriends. You can't tag along with them either. So I can find myself sitting in my flat phoning some of my mates in Glasgow and hoping that they'll be in.

Perhaps the best thing that could happen is for me to get married and settle down. I don't want the glamorous lifestyle that I'm supposed to enjoy so much. I don't want to be out at clubs all the time.

I don't intend to marry someone who is into high living because I don't want that for myself. Ideally I would like to marry a girl like my sister Janice. She isn't the most beautiful girl in the world, but she's very attractive and has a lovely personality. Also she's dead honest and knows what she wants from life; she's very down to earth. Someone like that would be good for me. Yes, someone like Janice would be perfect.

It may seem a contradiction when people try to equate what I'm saying with the pictures they've seen of me. Here with one girl, there with another; in Stringfellow's with Rod Stewart. I've enjoyed a few nights out, but they don't happen every week. Don't get me wrong – I love pretty girls, but I don't want someone who wants to go out on the town every night. That's not for me.

I'd like the kind of marriage that Paul Mariner has. Paul's one of my mates at Arsenal, and he always seems to be organizing things around his family. He always makes sure that the whole family is involved. That's the kind of marriage I would like. I come from a close family – we're still very close even though I'm down here and they're up in Glasgow – and that kind of background would give me the stability everyone needs.

It would help my career to be married. You can share problems with someone. You accept responsibility; there is an added dimension to your life. I'd like that. There would be more of a planned existence for me then. Right now I know the direction in which I would like to see my life going, but it would be better to share it with a wife and family.

I missed my family when I came south. Although I had my own house in Glasgow before I moved, I always knew that I could go across town to see my folks. It was hard to leave that, and it was even harder to leave my mates. There were five of us who were inseparable, really good mates. Besides Danny Crainie, Willie McStay and Mike Conroy, who were all at Celtic Park with me, there was my mate Bob (his real name is Peter Rae). We were always together. On a Friday night before a game they would came round and we would have a laugh, play records or watch videos.

Now on a Friday night in London I sit on my own thinking about the lads, and in the end pick up the phone and talk to them. But you may talk for ten or twenty minutes, and then you put the phone down and you're lonelier than ever.

There's not too much you can do about that. You can't go out all the time. And you certainly can't go into the West End very often because if you do your picture will appear in one of the gossip columns and everyone will think that you're cutting about town all the time. It is not like that. Going out two nights a week is my limit; in Glasgow I could be out most nights, except on the evening before a game.

Even my boss Don Howe had me in once after a few pictures had appeared in the newspapers. He asked me what was going on in my private life. He was probably beginning to believe that I was going out to clubs all the time. Sometimes I would go to a club on a Monday and the picture would only appear on the following Saturday morning, so people thought I'd been out the night before a match. Nothing could be farther from the truth. Anyhow I told Don that I was not going out much and that was true. I had stopped going to Stringfellow's, for example, because whenever I went in the door the flash bulbs were going. I need peace and quiet when I go out. I'd rather stay in than put up with that kind of hassle.

There was hassle in Glasgow, as well, but it was of a

different kind. My manager at Celtic, Billy McNeill, used to call me into the office in the mornings to check on what I'd been up to. Sometimes he had received letters or phone calls telling him this, that or the other. Most of the calls were to say that I'd been falling down drunk in some pub or club. In reality I'd probably been having a couple of pints of lager with my mates. Billy understood that. He was fantastic about it. He'd simply tell me to watch where I went when I was out. The problem was that everyone in Glasgow knew me, so it was a case of no hiding place!

Even so, it used to get me down. Anonymous phone calls to Celtic Park, poison pen letters to the manager, and, inevitably, problems over religion when I was out. Guys who were Rangers fans would want to fight with me at discos just because I happened to play for Celtic. When I left I thought I would leave all those worries behind me.

But London is no different except that it is more sophisticated. You have your picture taken in a night-club with some model or rock star, and that image hits many more people. Instead of a few spreading tales, thousands of people see the photographs or read the stories, and usually the stories are not very complimentary.

I like enjoying myself, I always have, ever since I grew up. When I was a kid I was really shy, especially with girls, believe it or not. My Mum tells me she used to get embarrassed because I'd never speak to anyone who came to the house. I've changed a bit since then, but I don't enjoy myself enough nowadays. In London I have to watch who I go out with. I have to watch what I'm having to drink. I have to watch where I go. Every single little thing has to be watched. It's very difficult to adjust to that. Instead of going out and relaxing a little, I go out and find that I'm giving myself headaches!

But there comes a time after a few weeks of staying in when I say to myself, 'Forget everybody and what

21

they're thinking, and just enjoy yourself.' It's necessary to do that occasionally because anyone in any job has to have some time to himself. Footballers need a chance to relax. It's only fair.

I've been criticized. Even my mate Graeme Souness suggested that I was living like a pop star. That's nonsense. I don't live like that at all. I train every day. I'm active every day of my life and there aren't many guys in the pop world who can say the same. And I love training. I am good at it; when it's hard I battle through. I never stop. I might not be up front leading the pack, but I'm not the last one in the group either. If I was living in the way Graeme seemed to think, then I wouldn't be able to do the kind of training we have at Arsenal. Don Howe would be able to spot it. Also it would show up in the weight check we have every Friday at Highbury. I've never had a weight problem. Right now my weight is steady at 11 stones 4 pounds. When I was at Celtic I was always around 10 stones 11 pounds. I'm only half a stone heavier now and that's due to the different kind of training that we do at Arsenal. It's added muscle more than anything else. Yet people go around saying that I'm heavy and that I've put on too much weight since I moved to London. It's just not true.

I admit that I've brought a lot of the criticism on my own head. When I first came down I was carried away by all the trappings of the career that people were predicting for me. I attracted the wrong kind of publicity. Jock Stein once told me that it was time I got my picture on the back pages instead of in the gossip columns, and he was right. I know that now and, deep down, I knew it then.

I've been embarrassed about some of the things which have happened. On one occasion I was supposed to have asked a punk heiress to pay for a date. An agency was responsible for that; they never even spoke to me about it. I felt terrible. That's the kind of thing that I don't want to get involved in. But at the time I was Jack the

Lad again so far as the public was concerned. I could have done without that.

Then there was the time when Samantha Fox and another of the *Sun*'s Page Three girls said I would be their ideal date. I know Samantha, she's a nice girl, but it's hard to handle that kind of publicity. My ambitions are to do well in the game and to help Arsenal win a trophy, and to get married and have a secure, stable family life. If I was running around with models all the time then I'd be cheating myself because I'd be selling short my own ambitions. I don't want all that.

I don't want to be lonely either, but if I have to be in order to run my life properly then that's how it goes. Forget all the happy snaps – football comes first. Just as it did when I was kicking a ball around as a kid.

3

How Celtic Let Me Down

It was the spring and summer of 1983 that the crunch time came with Celtic, the team I'd followed since I was a kid, the only team I'd ever wanted to play for. It still hurts when I look back at that time because I'm sure that the club wanted to sell me. The manager, Billy McNeill, wanted to keep me, I have no doubts about that, but I doubt whether all members of the board of directors wanted to hold on to me when they knew that they could cash in on a huge transfer fee from England. How else can you explain what they did? Day after day I woke up to headlines in the newspapers telling me that I was set to be the highest-paid player that Scotland had ever had. The club put out a great deal of propaganda to strengthen their position. I stayed silent, possibly because of the loyalty to Celtic that I'd felt since I was old enough to go to the games with my Dad.

The reality was far different from the stories handed out from Parkhead. The first offer made to me by Billy McNeill on behalf of the board was of £300 a week for a four-year contract. At that time there were four or five first-team players at Celtic who were making more money. And there were other players in Scotland – with Rangers, with Aberdeen and with Dundee United – who were on higher wages too. Yet the Celtic fans were conned into believing that I had been made a massive pay offer to stay with the club when my contract ended in the summer. Fans would come up to me in the street and say, 'You'll have to stay now that the club is being

24

so good to you.' I couldn't believe it. I made up my mind at that point that I had to move on.

I never made any demands on Celtic. Big Billy asked me what I was looking for but I genuinely didn't know what I wanted. In any case, it was up to the club to make me an offer. The ball was in their court. I had given them five years of my career and had cost them only a £200 signing-on fee when I could have taken £4000 from Bobby Robson at Ipswich. Surely that showed my feelings for the club? So I left them to make the offer, and £300 a week was all they came up with in the early negotiations.

The offer edged up after I had rejected the first few deals which had been proposed. But even at the end, when the final offer was outlined to me, it still didn't match up to the public statements the club was making. I still would not have been the best-paid player with Celtic. I certainly would not have been the best-paid player in Scotland – players with Aberdeen were on better money than I was being offered.

At the time, I didn't talk about the re-signing deal which was put to me. A sense of loyalty to Celtic stopped me. But I don't feel that loyalty now to the same extent. I'm convinced that the directors wanted to make money from my transfer.

Their last offer was a salary of £400 a week plus a signing-on fee of £20,000 spread over a four-year contract. That will seem a lot of money to guys who come from the same background as me, lads back in Glasgow who are on the dole or being paid terrible wages for jobs they don't even like. But for a footballer who has a short life, for someone who entertains the public, it was not a good offer. In fact, by English standards it was a lousy offer, and even in Scotland it wasn't all that bright!

There were ordinary players in England at that time, just good club players, who were making double that. Now, after a season in which I had scored 52 goals and forced my way into the international team, I was being

asked to take a much lower wage than I could get somewhere else. Not just for one year, either, but for *four*.
That is what I'd still be earning today if I had stayed
with Celtic.

People tried to persuade me to stay there. Billy
McNeill wanted to hold on to me. Frank Cairney, who
advised me during the negotiations, told me that I
should stay with the club. Frank knew where my heart
lay and, being such a strong Celtic man himself, he tried
to guide me to the decision which would have been best
for the club. But by then my mind was made up. If they
had made me a really good offer first time round,
perhaps I would have stayed. If they had done that and
kept the business between us private, I would have been
much more favourably inclined to the deal.

I took a fair bit of stick from the fans during that
spell. They'd remind me how they paid my wages and
how much I owed to Celtic. By that time I was looking
at things in an entirely different way from them. There's
no doubt that the fans pay your wages, but in my case
just a couple of hundred out of the average attendance
of maybe 26,000 were enough to do that. If I'd been
pushed to naming a price to stay I don't really know
what I would have had in mind. But after I had scored
all these goals it's probably fair to assume that perhaps
2000 fans were coming to see me every week. At that
time I was the favourite player of many of the fans
who went to Celtic Park week after week, so I may be
underestimating the number of people who wanted to
watch me scoring goals. Anyhow, even if there were only
2000, then surely I was going to be worth more than the
£300 or £400 a week that Celtic were prepared to give
me? As for owing Celtic – all I got when I signed for
them as a teenager was £200 and they sold me for three-
quarters of a million. Who came out best in that deal?

I loved Celtic. That's why I wanted to play for them
in the first place. I never thought about anything else
when I was a youngster. Even when I was in the reserves
and when I had made the first team I still went to the

terraces to cheer on the lads when I wasn't playing myself. Once at a European game, when I was just starting to push my way into the League side, I went to the 'Jungle' – the covered terracing opposite the main stand at Celtic Park – and joined the club's most fanatical supporters. I ended up in trouble with the manager for that. Big Billy McNeill gave me a rocket. I could have been sitting in the stand but I wanted to be there with the fans and feel the atmosphere again.

There was another time when I went to the terraces at Ibrox. It was the Glasgow Cup final and the two reserve sides were playing that night. So I went along with Danny Crainie and my kid brother Stephen to see my mate Willie McStay and give him a bit of support. As we were walking towards the ground I said to the others, 'C'mon, let's go to the terracing.' You should have seen the faces of the other supporters when they realized I was standing among them. At that time I was in the first team and was one of the top men. They couldn't believe their eyes. It wasn't a very important game but there were a few thousand there and they all seemed to be looking at me. My little brother was looking at me too; everyone was waiting to see what I was going to do when the singing started. So, naturally, I joined in, and that was it. What a good night we had – and Celtic won the Cup. The players came over to the Celtic end with the Cup and Willie was so surprised to see us standing there with the punters that he dropped the trophy!

Perhaps it was things like that, like going onto the terraces, that made it plain that I was Celtic-daft, so that the board believed that I would stay no matter what they offered me.

It's a sad fact that Celtic have taken advantage of their top players over the years. They haven't learned anything in their dealings with players. They are a great club to my mind, but the sadness lies in the way in which they have used people. The kind of players who have supported Celtic and been really loyal to the club have been the ones who have suffered most. I honestly believe that the board have played on players' loyalties. If they knew that someone cared deeply about the club then they seem to have expected him to stay on for low wages just to be able to say that he was a Celtic player. That doesn't work any more – but Celtic don't appear to have recognized it.

The players who have made most from Celtic are people like Frank Munro or Alfie Conn – and good luck to them, Alfie was a magic player – but they got more from the club than people who really loved Celtic. Kenny Dalglish, Tommy Burns and others have given more to the club, but somehow the club doesn't give back to you what you put into it. You are taken for granted. It's as if the club says, 'Well, he loves Celtic, so he'll stay.'

I was deeply involved in supporting Celtic from the time I was a kid. Not only did my Dad take me to the games, he used to teach me songs about the old teams and players. He'd tell me about the League Cup final when Celtic beat Rangers 7–1 and Sammy Wilson and Billy McPhail destroyed the Rangers centre half John Valentine. He'd tell me about how Celtic won the Coronation Cup in 1953, when Neilly Mochan, who was a coach at the Park when I was there, was the star. The late Jock Stein used to look at that cup in the Celtic boardroom and call it 'Mochan's Cup'. I had books about the club and books by the players, like Tommy Gemmell's *The Big Shot*. I was reared believing that the club was the greatest in the world, and many other players went through the same as I did when they were schoolkids. You used to pride yourself on how much you knew about the club and how much you could hear about the players who had been with the club in the past. My Dad used to tell me about Charlie Tully, for example, how he scored direct from a corner at Falkirk one day, had to retake the kick and did the same again, and how Tully used to try to take corners from the edge of the 18-yard line when the ref wasn't paying attention.

It is for things like that that he is still remembered by the supporters, even by the fans who are too young to have seen him.

The stories about Tully might have influenced my attitude to the game. Football should be fun and the players have to get the fans involved. It's not all solemn and dull. It's something to be enjoyed by everyone – by those watching from the terraces and by the lads out on the field. Bertie Auld did outrageous things, like sitting on the ball during a game against Clyde. You don't see anything like that now and the game is the poorer because of it.

I owe Celtic a lot. The club kindled my ambitions to play the game and gave me the chance to make it as a professional. I'll always be grateful for that. In the reserves I had Frank Connor watching over me. He kicked me up the backside when he thought that I needed it and praised me when he felt that I deserved it. In between he worked me very hard, but he got it right. I'd been the last of the young crop of players to get into the reserve team, but I was the first to break through into the League side. A lot of the credit for that goes to Frank.

He realized what I needed. He recognized me as a person in my own right, not just as one of the young players who were trying to break through. I needed that kind of recognition and a little bit of encouragement at the appropriate time. Even when I was scoring bundles of goals for the reserves he still took time out to make me work hard at my game. He impressed upon me that things don't come easily when you are a professional.

Then Frank handed me on to Billy McNeill, and he was a lot like Jock Stein when it came to finding exactly the right time for me to take the next step in my career. Just as Big Jock didn't push me into the international side straightaway, but took his time to pick the right kind of game for me to make my debut, so Billy did the same when it came to the Celtic first team. Billy could have taken the gamble with me earlier but I'm glad he didn't. He watched my progress with the reserves, saw me coming to a peak and then, just at the time I felt that I was ready to make it in the Premier League, he pushed me in. If I had gone in a little bit earlier I might have found it too difficult and that could have set my career back a few months or even longer. If he had waited a few months more I could easily have been so sick at not getting a chance that my game might have gone off the boil. He knew exactly when I should hit the first team. His timing was perfect, and I appreciated that then and appreciate it just as much now.

It's not easy for managers to know how to handle players all the time, and I accept that I can be a little bit difficult. The way Billy nursed me into the first team was important for me then. Just as it was when it came to the Scotland team. Big Jock was under pressure to play me because I was getting goals for Celtic, but he didn't want me to make my debut away from home, where I might not be getting too many passes made to me up front, and where the result might go against us. He maintained that the best place for me to start my international career was at Hampden. He picked me to play against Switzerland there, I scored a really good goal, and I hope that proved to everyone how right the Big Man had been. I don't think I could have picked a better game for myself than that one.

These little things may not seem important to anyone outside the game, but they are vital to players, particularly young players, who tend to be impatient. When you are a teenager trying to make a name for yourself, there are times when you believe that you're better than you really are. Times when you reckon you should be in the first team when you are still just serving your apprenticeship. Proper handling in your teens or early twenties can make you a better player later in life.

Eighteen months before my contract with Celtic ended I was ready to ask for a transfer simply because I had lost my first-team place. I had had one good season, then the next year George McCluskey got back into the side when I was injured. He played well and stayed there with Frank McGarvey, while I was back in the reserves or sometimes on the bench. I wasn't pleased and asked my sister to type out a succession of transfer requests for me. I didn't tell my parents; I only told Janice – because I wanted the letters typed – and Danny McGrain, who gave me advice.

Danny thought that I should wait, be patient, but in the end he told me that I had to make up my own mind about something that was so important. So, after tearing up several requests as I agonized about what I should do, I decided to hand the letter in to Billy McNeill. A few days before D-day I broke my leg playing for the reserves at Greenock. Was I glad that I hadn't been able to make up my mind earlier! The letter was torn up and I spent virtually the rest of the season on the treatment table at Parkhead.

That is the worst injury I've ever had and it happened when I went into a tackle with Joe McLaughlin, who is now with Chelsea but was then with Morton. The conditions were bad that night at Cappielow. I had beaten a couple of players to get into the box, when Joe raced in to challenge. He caught me badly and down I went. I knew the leg was broken, but it wasn't Joe's fault. I didn't blame him at the time and I don't blame him now.

The injury caused an unscheduled pause in my career but it also stopped me from asking to leave too soon. The right time to move was when my contract ended. Staying on then would have been just as wrong as asking for a transfer when I had lost my place in the League side.

Since I left, there has been talk about my going back to Celtic, but that will never happen. Returning to Celtic would be moving backwards. There is no way that I want to do that. There were rumours that I would go back simply because I found it hard-going at Highbury. People know how much I still care for the club, but I care for Arsenal too. Playing at Highbury has opened

31

my eyes to a lot of things. For instance, back home in Glasgow you grow up thinking of Celtic and Rangers as really top clubs. And they are. But Arsenal is one of the world's great teams. Nor could I return to the parochial atmosphere of Glasgow. I've had my problems in London but the homesickness disappeared a long time ago and I've adjusted to the different lifestyle.

I wouldn't be happy playing for a club who let me down in the end. That offer the directors made to me still rankles. Celtic seem to have learned very little over the years about how to keep their star players happy. From the time Kenny Dalglish left until the time I left six years or so later their attitude hadn't changed. It was almost as if they were doing us a favour by letting us wear that green and white jersey. They still felt they were bestowing an honour on us by allowing us to play for the club we supported. That's an attitude which went out years ago in most clubs.

It still persists at Celtic but they will soon have to realize that they are in the 1980s and that players have to be treated properly. If they don't do that, then they will continue to lose their best players either to England or to the Continent. Loyalty has to work both ways.

4

Transfer Tug-of-War

The news that I was to leave Celtic came in May 1983 when I saw the club chairman, the late Desmond White, and formally turned down the contract they had offered me. That was it. There was no way back and, to be honest, I didn't want one. All I wanted was to concentrate on the British international championship games which were looming, along with a close-season tour of Canada with the Scotland international team. But instead of being able to concentrate on my game as I tried to establish myself in the Scottish side, I found myself at the centre of a transfer tug-of-war which almost pulled me to pieces!

Three of Britain's biggest clubs wanted me to sign for them. I had the kind of choice that every schoolboy dreams about: I could opt for Liverpool, Manchester United or Arsenal. And if for some unaccountable reason I didn't fancy them, then I could take a look at what Inter Milan or Torino of Italy had on offer for me.

It was an unbelievable few weeks as I tried to assess all of the offers and make up my mind which move would be the most advantageous for me and for my career. Everyone was offering advice. Everyone seemed to know what would be best for me. The trouble was that 'everyone' wasn't going to make the decision. I had to do that by myself. It was in a hotel room in Vancouver that I finally plumped for Arsenal. Put like that, it sounds so easy. But that sentence hides three weeks of turmoil as I weighed up the different offers.

First of all I dismissed the offers which had reached

me from Italy. I was too young to go over there and try
to make a career for myself in strange surroundings.
There were temptations, as there were with all the offers,
but not sufficient to lure me out of the country. Financially it would have been sensational for me. It would
also have meant that I was playing alongside some of
the greatest players in the world. Brazilians, Argentin-
ians, the Italians themselves, stars such as Michel Platini
of France and Liam Brady and Trevor Francis, who had
gone out to Sampdoria. There were things that appealed
to me, but I knew I would have problems settling –
problems with the language, problems with the very
different way of life. If I had been a few years older and
married then it might have been a possibility. But I
wasn't, and so the Italian job was a non-starter even
though the offer would have made me a very rich young
man. Indeed, I would never have had financial worries
in my life again.

The first club I met was Liverpool. I had talks with
the chairman John Smith, the secretary Peter Robinson
and Bob Paisley. From that moment on I realized how
difficult the choice of club was going to be. All of them
were top clubs. Initially I had thought I would like to
join Manchester United. They are such a glamorous
club and there has always been a certain kinship between
them and Celtic down through the years. And I don't
think there is a bigger stage in Britain than Old Trafford
for players to parade their skills. But the opening round
of talks with Liverpool began to put doubts into my
mind. They were all such down-to-earth people, men
who talked good sense, and I still needed that kind of
solid experience to guide me.

As well as that, of course, Graeme Souness and Kenny
Dalglish were there. It seemed perfect in a way for me
to follow Kenny, play with him and learn from him and
yet part of me doubted the wisdom of the move, doubted,
really, the wisdom of trying to follow Kenny. In the end
Kenny, my idol and now the Liverpool manager, was
the number one reason why I didn't go to Anfield!

I admired the way he had moved from Celtic to take over from Kevin Keegan. No one was supposed to be able to replace Keegan at that time, although any Celtic supporter could have told the lads on the Kop that they were getting the best of the deal. I don't mean any disrespect to Kevin, but when it comes to natural ability, something that footballers look for first, he simply isn't in the same class as Kenny in my eyes. He worked very hard and he did well for himself, but Kenny is a different animal altogether. In a way it was easy for Kenny to follow Keegan because he was a better player. But it wasn't going to be easy to follow Kenny. There was no way that I believed that I could do that.

I wasn't worried about my ability. But Kenny had already taken over from one Liverpool legend and, being Kenny, had turned himself into an even bigger legend. Greatness stops at a certain level; to try to take on two legends in succession looked too much for me. Perhaps some day in the future someone will be able to outdo Kenny – but I didn't see it then, and I don't really see it happening now. Anyhow, it wasn't a job that I fancied risking my reputation on. Basically I felt that it was too much for me to take on as a twenty-one-year-old.

Both Kenny and Graeme tried to persuade me that Liverpool was the club to join – especially Graeme – but deep down the presence of Kenny and all he had done was the killer. I couldn't handle that.

After the talks with Liverpool it was on to talks with Manchester United, the club which was first choice in my own mind. Also it was first choice among most of the fans following the transfer saga throughout that week of the British international championship. In Glasgow even the bookies were offering odds on my final destination, with United edging slightly ahead of Liverpool and Arsenal running in third place.

In the beginning the clubs were in that position so far as I was concerned. Obviously Arsenal was a club I respected a great deal for its tradition, for its history, for all the wonderful achievements in the past. The other two were different – Liverpool were the *best* team in the country and United were the *biggest* team in the country.

Somehow, though, in United's talks with me they didn't come over in the way I expected. I met only Ron Atkinson and Martin Edwards. We all know about Ron. Perhaps some young players are impressed when they see the guy with his expensive suits and all that gold jewellery, but it didn't do a whole lot for me. Neither did Martin Edwards, particularly compared with the Liverpool delegation. He was sincere enough, as was Ron, but they didn't convince me in the way the Liverpool people did. Everything about the men from Anfield was direct. There were no airs or graces, and they had Bob Paisley with them. He didn't say a lot, but what he did say made sense immediately.

I didn't get that impression from United in the two or three meetings I had with them. They weren't able to say where they wanted me to play. Or how they wanted me to play. Or even if they would be guaranteeing me a place in their first team! That didn't make sense, especially as they were prepared to lay out almost a quarter of a million pounds to buy me. Nothing about the meetings seemed right and I had gone into them looking for the chance to join United. I was disappointed, saddened, and more than a little disillusioned.

Yet if they had done one thing, just one simple thing, I would have signed for them. All they had to do was ask Sir Matt Busby to talk to me and I would have joined them straightaway. They had one of the greatest names in football on the board, the man who had built the club, and yet I never had the chance to meet him. While the negotiations were going on the only people I met were Martin Edwards and Ron Atkinson. Making a big move like that, I wanted to see other people, perhaps talk to someone else from the boardroom who could give another insight into the club's plans or views. It didn't happen, and so I began to doubt United.

If Sir Matt had come along I would have found it much easier to link the people talking to me with the club that every football-playing schoolboy dreams about. He was Manchester United. He was also a Scot – and that would have helped me feel at ease – and he was someone I wanted to meet, someone I had total respect for, someone I knew would give me sound advice. A few words from Sir Matt, and I would have been signing forms without worrying too much about the wages. That's how much influence he would have had over me. I'm surprised, even now, that he was not brought along to some of the talks.

Liverpool impressed me more than United; they always appeared to be one step ahead. But in spite of the impressive meetings with them and the obvious sincerity of Bob Paisley, there was still Kenny and that reputation of his lying in wait for me at Anfield. That's when Arsenal arrived on the scene, and Terry Neill, their manager at that time, and his assistant Don Howe, who is now the club's boss, convinced me where my future lay.

The day after playing for Scotland against England at Wembley I met them in the Park Lane Hotel in London. It wasn't long before they started to make a distinct impression on me. Arsenal are a big club and they were desperate for success; they felt that I could help them get that. The scenario they outlined was attractive. They were saying, more or less, that they had to awaken a sleeping giant and get Arsenal back among the honours and back into Europe. They told me that I was the kind of player they wanted to help them do that. That was a boost in itself, being told straight out how much they wanted me and why they wanted me. They had plans for the club and I was going to be part of them. The sense of challenge attracted me from the very start of our talks. Maybe people will think I'm contradicting myself because Terry Neill and Don Howe were the only two representatives from Arsenal that I met. But they were football people and that was important.

Up to that day all the signs had been that the choice

lay between Liverpool and United. I'd met them both
and been left with worries over both. Meeting up with
Arsenal was refreshing. There was no Dalglish from
whom I would have to take over, and the management
team spelled out how much they wanted to make me
part of their future. For all the big talk, United had not
been able to do that.

Terry Neill was very persuasive, very charming and
a great talker. I liked him a lot, but I had been told
before the meeting that Don Howe as assistant was
responsible for most of the decisions on the playing side
and so I listened to him very carefully too. Don came
over as a very honest person. He was the key man at
those talks. It was probably due more to Don than to
Terry that I signed for the Arsenal.

I didn't make my decision right away, although the
thought of joining Arsenal was growing firmer in my
mind after that London meeting. At the time all I
wanted was a break from the hectic dashing around
which had taken my mind off football too much during
the home championship. The Scotland manager Jock
Stein hadn't been too happy about the whole thing, and
I can't blame him. In the little village of Harpenden
before the England game I was being whisked by Mer-
cedes from one meeting to another. Football was the last
thing on my mind for part of that time. The chance to
get back home to Glasgow for a few days to talk things
over with my parents seemed an ideal break.

I had only a few days there before I was off to Canada
with Scotland for a tour of three international games –
in Vancouver, Edmonton and Toronto. I had to make
my decision early in the tour to avoid any repeat of the
transfer circus which had distracted me at home. A
couple of days into the trip, while we were staying in a
luxury hotel in Vancouver, I decided on Arsenal.
Funnily enough, on tour with a team you don't always
get a chance to be on your own to think things out. This
time I did get the opportunity. For once I wasn't sharing
a room because my room-mate Graeme Souness, the

Liverpool skipper, was in the Far East with his club during the first part of our tour. Terry Neill phoned me from Djakarta, where he was on tour with Arsenal, and that was the only interruption I had.

I went over in my mind all the pros and cons, and although I hadn't sat down to work out the financial aspects of each deal I knew that there was not very much between them. The important thing was picking the *right* club for the *right* reasons. Arsenal weren't going to be playing in Europe the following season, and after my years with Celtic that would be something that I would miss desperately. Nor had they been able to match their history with their present achievements; winning trophies didn't happen as often as at Anfield. There would be the inevitable comparisons made between myself and Peter Marinello, the one-time Arsenal winger, who joined them from Hibs and failed to make a real impression with the club. His career at Highbury ended with accusations that he had enjoyed London's night life a little too much for his own and the team's good. I believed that I could handle the last problem and I believed, equally, that the others could be taken care of. There were good players at Highbury and there were suggestions that other good players would be arriving for the new season.

There was an excitement in all this which I didn't get from the other two choices open to me. I felt that I was going to be a part of something really big, the rebirth of a great Arsenal team. Just thinking about this gave me a buzz.

And there was a secret bonus on offer at that time. During the talks there had been expressed the underlying belief, shared by Terry and Don, that Liam Brady was going to return from Italy and rejoin Arsenal. That had been spelled out to me and it was another aspect of the move which excited me a great deal. 'Chippy' Brady was the player who had been vitally important to Arsenal when they had had their previous run of success. He was the perfect midfield general and everything that

39

I knew about him, both from seeing him play and from what I had heard about him from other players, made me feel that we would be on the same wavelength. When we have played together in various testimonial matches that has been the case. He has guided me through things because that's the way the fellow plays. He is the type of player all forwards would like to be able to link up with. In a sense he reminds me of Kenny Dalglish; he would never land another player in trouble if he could avoid it. By that I mean that he would rather be caught in possession himself than give a forward the ball when the pass isn't on. You appreciate that in a fellow professional perhaps more than anything else.

He plays the game the way I've always wanted to play it. He's ready to play one–twos in the instinctive way that Tommy Burns and I used to do at Celtic. It is something that comes naturally, and Chippy has an innate ability to assess situations and adapt to them. The times I have played with him have been a joy for me. They have given me a taste of how things might have been at Arsenal if he had come home to Highbury. The fans would have liked that too. It would have been a dream partnership, and from what Liam has said to me I think he would have enjoyed it too. I'm disappointed that it didn't work out. For myself mainly. For Arsenal. And for those fans on the North Bank who adopted me so readily and who have always adored Liam. I still harbour hopes that I will team up with him some day.

I didn't tell anyone when I finally made up my mind to join Arsenal. In fact I didn't tell anyone on the tour party. The first person I spoke to was Ken Gallacher, the sports writer with the Sun who has helped me write this book. After that I phoned home to tell my folks. I was prepared to take some stick for the choice I had made when the news broke at home the following day. Jock Stein didn't think I had made the right move. He had been in favour of Liverpool when I'd talked with him because he felt that their discipline and professionalism would be good for me and my career. But although he said that he was disappointed he wished me good luck. The real stick came when Graeme arrived from Liverpool's tour. Jet-lagged or not after a trip which had taken him halfway round the world, he ripped into me. He had always been strong about my joining up at Anfield – much more so than Kenny had been – and let me know what he thought. I don't think Graeme has ever plugged Liverpool so much in his life. He had been biting my ear throughout the transfer talks and then when he found out that I had plumped for Arsenal he was very angry. I tried to explain to him that there was no way I could follow in Kenny's footsteps, but that didn't impress him. He thought, like Jock Stein, that Liverpool was the best place for me.

Graeme's opinion more than any other made the decision difficult for me. I have a great deal of respect for him and for his views on the game, so it was hard to go against him. But I couldn't allow myself to be influenced by anyone – this was a personal decision and no one could make it except me. I accepted a great deal of what Graeme and Jock Stein said. I knew as well as they did that I still had things to learn about the game. You get so far on natural skill but you have to be able to add more than that, and I felt that Arsenal could teach me the next few steps as well as anyone else could. Adding another layer of professionalism to my game and to my approach was a priority. But this could be done at Highbury under Don Howe just as easily as at Liverpool under Joe Fagan. That was something I was always prepared for. There was no way that I was arriving in London thinking that, at twenty-one years of age, I knew it all. I didn't. And I still don't. This game is one in which the learning process can go on throughout your career. Having natural ability had carried me so far, but I was well aware that it wouldn't necessarily take me any farther.

The English First Division offers many problems for players, particularly forwards, and particularly forwards who arrive with goal-scoring credentials. I didn't realize just how hard the transition from being a success with Celtic to becoming a success with Arsenal would be. Nor how long it was going to take. The lessons ahead were to be painful ones.

5

Settling in with Arsenal

On the day I signed for Arsenal, clinching the decision I'd reached in Canada, I made it clear that I still considered that I was a learner in the game. Both Terry Neill and Don Howe had impressed on me the differences between the English First Division and the Scottish Premier League. They had stressed that I had to give total application to the game. Also I had to become part of the team plan. So when the press came to cover the actual signing of my new contract I told everyone that I was going to try to forget individualism, that I had to try to emulate someone like Kevin Keegan in his approach to the game, build my professionalism and become a player within a team. At Celtic I'd been given scope to express myself, a great deal more freedom than most players in England would ever be allowed. That had worked for me: I had scored more than 50 goals in the previous season, but such a carefree approach might not be what Arsenal needed from me if they were to get the success they wanted. It seemed so simple at the time. On that June morning I could scarcely wait for the season to begin and for my new career to take off. However, that's not the way it turned out and there are many reasons for that.

I don't want to hide behind excuses for all the things that have gone wrong. Some of the fault is mine, but some of it has to rest with the general situation at Arsenal. My pride has been hurt, there is no getting away from that. I'd had a few hiccups in my career before I moved south. There were a couple of times

when I was dropped by Celtic, and when I broke my
leg I couldn't get straight back into the team because
Frank McGarvey and George McCluskey had paired up
so well together in my absence. But in the main I had
tasted success in almost all those years playing with the
Celtic first team. And when I'd been dropped I knew
that when I got back in the team I would be returning
to one that was challenging for honours – and winning
them too – a team that was charged with the kind of
confidence that only a run of victories can provide.

Sadly, that has never been the case in my time with
Arsenal. It has been the same ever since I joined the
club: you go out of the team when the manager wants
to try something else or someone else, and then, when
you get back, you find the same old problems are there.
People at the club keep looking back. They'll talk about
the old double team of fifteen years ago. Or they'll hark
back to the last team to win the FA Cup in 1979, when
Frank Stapleton and Liam Brady were the stars. The
ghosts of these players seem to stalk the marble halls of
Highbury and I doubt if they will ever be laid to rest
until the present team can win some major trophy.

However, that is a general problem, part of the background which affects every player at the club. I have
had my own specific problems, and although I arrived
willing to learn new things about the game, my own
particular skills have suffered in the process. For
example, I've been shunted back and forward between
different roles in the team. For one spell I was playing
up front, then I was back in midfield, then I was floating
in behind the two main strikers, then I was back up
front again. There have been times when I didn't know
where I was – and I've said so. At other times I wasn't
able to concentrate on the things I'm good at – like
scoring goals – because I'd been asked to do something
else. So I would find myself in midfield trying to create
openings for Tony Woodcock or Paul Mariner, and when
a half chance came to me – the kind of opening which
had brought me goals at Celtic – I'd be caught in two

44

minds. I'd see the chance but I'd be aware that the role
I had been handed was to provide chances for others.
When you experience that kind of momentary indecision
opportunities are lost.

Goals come when you react swiftly and instinctively.
Goals come when you provide the unexpected finish to
a move, when you do something out of the ordinary and
surprise the opposition. That's what I was good at.
That's why, I believed, Arsenal had bought me. Then I
found out that they didn't want anything too unorthodox
and so I tried to conform. In doing that I was caught
between two stools. There I was, struggling to be the
normal, thoroughly professional First Division footballer, when in reality I was wanting to kick over the
traces and do something on my own. It's this problem
which we have never been able to resolve.

Don thought for a while that I could be the new
Michel Platini. He didn't want me tied down to being
solely a penalty-box player. So I went deep and tried to
play that role, but I was never truly happy there. It was
uncomfortable. It wasn't a natural way for me to be
playing.

There was a spell when Don would take me into his
office – just him and me – and show me tapes. Every
time it was Platini we were watching. And Don would
say, 'Watch him, because this is the player you could
be. If your ability likens you to anyone, then it's to
him.' I'd come out thinking, how can I do this? How
can I match the player who is arguably the best in the
world?

I've watched Platini on the telly playing for Juventus
and it's amazing how all the rest of the team try to give
him the ball. There they are, the team of all the talents,
and yet they still look for him whenever one of them has
gained possession. He runs the show. He is the gaffer. I
remember, particularly, watching Platini in the Super
Cup game against Liverpool in Turin. He ran that game.
Whenever Juventus got into the Liverpool half of the
field they looked to him to give them their lead. It

was as though they were asking themselves, 'Where's Platini?' Of course, he was always making himself available and so they would always give him the ball. Liverpool were under a lot of pressure.

He can also do special things with the ball. He makes mistakes, every player does, but it's the little telling things that he produces that really count. It doesn't matter whether he has a marker or not because he will drop deep and look for the ball there. For part of the game he might not cause any damage; he'll seem content to wait for his chance. When he goes deep he sits there in his own half and knocks little passes around, the way he did in the European championship final for France against Spain when they tried to mark him out of the game. He has the knack of lulling the opposition into thinking that he is out of the action. They see him hitting a few simple passes almost on top of his own back four and so they forget about him. Then, when they have stopped checking on him, maybe for just a minute, he will move upfield, getting himself in there behind them where he *can* cause trouble.

The marvellous thing about him is the way he can run teams. He runs Juventus and he runs France, and the other players seem happy with that arrangement. I don't think that could happen to the same extent in British football.

It's the greatest compliment possible that Don should compare me to Platini. It's a sign of just how much Don wants to help me, how much he wants me to make it at Arsenal. However, I've never based my style on him, not even when Don was saying that I could be another Platini. It wouldn't work out for me. No one is going to alter the whole pattern of a team just to fit round me. That's what they do with him.

Yet I know that I can do some of the things that he does. I've watched him so many times on the video and I've come away saying to myself, 'You can do that.' It's not running the show that I'm talking about, it's some of the passes he makes, some of the ways he can beat a man, some of the goals he scores. I know that I can match him in these things.

But Don has tried to get more than that into my game. He has stressed that I must not allow myself to be pushed around on the park. Don's right, but it's something I'm not used to. I've always been kicked – as a forward you learn to expect that – but in the past I always shrugged it off. But Don wants me to let defenders know that I'm not going to be an easy mark. He wants me to show more aggression in these situations.

Don has tried very hard to help me since I joined the club. He has encouraged me and worked with me and that's meant a lot. At the same time I know deep within myself that there is nothing he can do to improve my skills. They are natural. I've always had them. Ever since I can remember kicking a ball about in the streets of Glasgow I've had the kind of individual skills that I still have today. But there isn't the opportunity to show them off as much during games.

People say that Don isn't comfortable with me because I'm a maverick. Maybe there's some truth in that, but Don was the man who really persuaded me to join Arsenal and he has given me lots of encouragement in the time we have been working together. On one occasion, at Watford in a game we won 4–3, I had one of my best games since coming to Arsenal. Yet after the game Don scarcely spoke to me and I wondered what was happening. But then he came up ever so quietly while I was getting my boots off, tapped me on the shoulder and said, 'Well done, I'm really pleased for you.' It may not seem much but it was enough to make me feel good and to let me know that Don cared about how I was doing. He doesn't have favourite players or anything like that, but a little word here and there lets you know he cares.

He has had a lot of unfair criticism. While Terry Neill was still Arsenal manager, and since he took over as manager himself, Don has been hammered by the press

47

and the fans. It makes me laugh when guys come up and tell me how defensive Don is. How he will never let teams really attack. How all he wants is a team built on a dull system designed not to lose goals.

That's a load of rubbish! Don Howe is not the high priest of defensive football that the public believes he is. It's almost as if he were as bad as Helenio Herrera, whose tactics did so much damage to the game in the sixties when the Italians retreated behind their sweepers. Don is not like that. I cannot understand how he was saddled with that reputation.

Just as any manager, he likes to have the defence organized. Certain things go through his mind, certain points will worry him but everyone worries about losing goals. When we're with Scotland even Kenny Dalglish says if we don't lose any goals we have a chance. He is one of the most attack-minded players in the country, in the world, and he's making that kind of statement. If Don were to say the same thing it would be interpreted as preaching the dullest of dull defensive play, yet no one would ever accuse Kenny of that attitude.

Essentially I think that people misunderstand Don. It has not been an easy job for him and it wasn't made any easier when Terry Neill was sacked about six months after I joined the club. That was a shock for me – and a blow because I liked Terry Neill a lot. He was the man who had bought me and I'll always be grateful to him for that. And he kept faith with me in those early months when I was finding it so hard to settle down and play in the way they wanted me to play. The goals everyone expected never arrived. They dried up, just as can happen with any striker, and the harder I tried to shake off the worries about my form the worse they affected my game. It was a miserable time for me because I was really intent on succeeding. I wanted to show what I could do in the First Division. I wanted to repay Arsenal for buying me and to give those fans on the North Bank something extra to shout about.

But things didn't go right for me, and because I was

One of the European games Charlie recalls – a victory at Parkhead against Real
Sociedad. Here he is challenged by Spanish defender, Ignatio Cortabarria

Hearts veteran Sandy Jardine, the former Rangers and Scotland star, is left
stranded as he goes to challenge Charlie in full flight

Above left: Player of the Year for the Scottish Football Writers' Association in 1983, his last season with Celtic

Above right: Billy McNeill, the man who brought Charlie into the Celtic first team and guided his early career

Above: Arsenal line up to salute the Celtic fans at Parkhead in a pre-season friendly following Charlie's transfer – but Charlie was rewarded with jeers from the Glasgow fans

Right: Former teammate Roy Aitken moves in to challenge Charlie on that return visit

Left: More scoring action from Charlie in his Celtic days, this time against Motherwell as Joe Carson comes in too late to block Charlie's shot

Above: A penalty goal for Charlie against Wolves in an English first division clash

Below left: Arsenal boss Don Howe supported by Charlie over the charges from critics that he is too defensive

Below right: Liam Brady, the Highbury hero Charlie would love to team up with

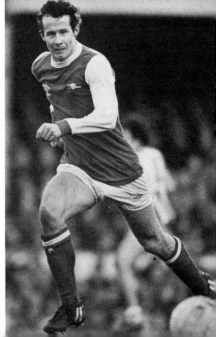

concentrating so hard on my own problems I was taken by surprise when the news came in December that Terry was leaving the club. Clearly he had been under pressure because the results had not been going the way the board expected them to go. But I didn't have the least inkling that he was going to be axed. Strangely enough, the talk in the dressing room that morning was that Don Howe would go too. So far as the players were concerned, Don had been the boss. He had taken the training, worked out the tactics, so it looked as if he would go with Terry. Yet he stayed, and that season he turned us around a little and had us playing open, exciting, attacking football. I was impressed by the way he did that. It showed enormous strength of character to come in and make the changes he did while most of the football world thought he was simply on trial for the job of manager.

Terry's sacking upset me. Some sources suggested that one of the reasons he had gone was because of my disappointing form after he had paid out so much money for me. That was nonsense; it was the general situation at the club that came to a head.

Terry is a gentleman and maybe that isn't exactly the right credential for a successful football manager. He is a genuinely pleasant person, the kind of man who will listen to you if you have a problem. He *really* listens. It's not a case of going in one ear and out of the other. Terry takes a sincere interest in people. He's a very honest, down-to-earth guy.

As a manager, he was the same – nice and easy and pleasant – and although he could knock a player when he wanted to, it was nothing like some managers could do. He would say something to a player in the same tone of voice as he would use to say hello in the morning when he came into the dressing room before training. There was nothing domineering, nothing commanding about him. After being with managers like Jock Stein and Billy McNeill I was surprised by that. They had a different approach. If they wanted to get a point across there would be an edge to their voices. They talked a little louder than when passing the time of day. You knew without any question that they were being serious about the subject in hand. Terry wasn't like that at all. He seemed too soft with certain players in certain situations.

For example, he never wanted to be called 'Boss'. He wanted the players to call him 'Terry' and that even became 'Tel' at times. It was not the way I had been brought up. No one would ever call Jock Stein anything other than Boss, and the same went for Big Billy. You called them Boss as a mark of respect, and yet here was Terry Neill dispensing with that very obvious sign of rank. I didn't like it. It made me feel uncomfortable and in some cases it brought him less respect from players than he deserved.

I don't know why he didn't want to be called Boss. Perhaps it was because he knew some of the other players from when he had been playing himself, like Pat Jennings and David O'Leary. It was as if he was still trying to be one of the lads, but when you become a manager you can't do that. Managers have to change and Terry didn't change from how he had been as a player. Perhaps he felt it was the best approach, but when I arrived at the club there were certain players who had no respect for him at all. I respected him, but there was that softness which bothered me.

He appeared to be the same during the week as he was after we had suffered a bad defeat. He cared in a way that wasn't obvious and he had a great love for the club, a deep affection for Arsenal that still surfaces. He still comes to Highbury most weeks to watch us. Possibly he now realizes that he should have been a little bit stronger, a little bit harder, especially with certain players at the club. His only fault was being too lenient with some of the lads and it cost him his job in the end.

Yet I don't know what he could have done about the situation at the club. It was at a low, and that was the result of things being wrong for some time. There was a lack of morale in the dressing room. The lads all got on well enough – they're a lovely bunch of fellows to have at any club – but it was as if some of us were just going through the motions. We needed someone to sort us out and say, 'Right, let's start from here and this is the way we can get things right.' But no one ever said that. No one seemed able to put his finger on what was wrong with the team and the performances. We thought that if we just kept working then we would get by, but the problem was too big, too deep-rooted. Tinkering wasn't going to bring about the changes and the success that the directors and the supporters wanted.

I was upset when Terry went, but that wasn't true of all the players. In the dressing room that morning there were one or two who were quite happy that he had been sacked. They never batted an eyelid when the news reached us. Probably everyone felt sad for Terry the man – he is the kind of person you cannot dislike. But so far as Terry the manager was concerned a few couldn't see him out of the job quickly enough. Perhaps they thought that a managerial change would work the little miracle we were all waiting for. That was the main reason they were quite happy about his departure. It was the same players who didn't give him respect when he was boss who didn't give a damn about him when he was sacked. Yet they were probably a little to blame for what happened.

I've met Terry a few times since he left and he seems to be getting on well. I'm sure that deep down he was hurt at losing the job. I knew he had a special feeling for Arsenal even though I'd only been with the club six months. Maybe it would have been different if the other players had recognized that.

Don has been harder on us than Terry ever was. There was one game in which we played badly and he lashed us in the newspapers. He said that we should be ashamed to pick up our wages that week – and he was right. We didn't play well. We let him down and he was perfectly entitled to have a go at us.

Don Howe is the best coach I know. There are people

who say that Terry Venables is the top man – Kenny Sansom, who was with Terry for a while, rates him highly – but for me Don is the number one. There's no one to beat Don as a coach in my eyes. He's not charismatic but that doesn't matter because he is so good at his job. However, if he could sell himself a little better, it might help him to fend off some of the unfair criticism.

Don deserves a lot more credit for his contribution to the game than he ever receives. Ask any player who has worked with him and you'll get the same answer; none of them would call him defensive. It's just not true.

6

My Love Affair with the North Bank

Since 1983 the decision to join Arsenal has caused me all kinds of hassle off the field. Not at Highbury itself, where everyone has been fine, but around the country. I've found myself booed by the Kop, jeered by Manchester United supporters and dropped from Scotland's World Cup team.

I've also been hounded by football writers who wanted me to admit that I'd made a mistake in that summer of 1983. Well, in one way I did make the wrong choice. I'm totally envious of Liverpool and Manchester United. I'm particularly envious of Liverpool because of the honours that they have won. I have to be honest with myself and privately I've admitted that to Graeme Souness and Kenny Dalglish when we have talked things over. To be fair, they've never rubbed it in, but they've said, 'We told you Arsenal would struggle a little.' I have had to agree that's what has happened. They were right and I was wrong. But I'm still happy with Arsenal in spite of all the problems we have had.

My contract still has some time left to run. I signed for four years and if within that time Arsenal collect a major honour then I'll reckon that I was right. It's not the kind of decision that can be judged over the first year or two. It has to be looked at in the context of my whole career. It may seem wrong at the moment, but there is still time for everything to come out right for me. If a top trophy ends up at Highbury then it will mean more than being part of a prizewinning Liverpool or Manchester United team. They always seem to be among the honours, while Highbury has been without anything since that Cup victory in 1979. It would be a tremendous achievement if I could help the club move back among the top teams in the country again. There's no doubt in my mind that that is where Arsenal deserve to be.

The tradition that exists in the club has great influence. You walk into the front hall and the bust of Herbert Chapman and the club's insignia in marble hit you smack between the eyes. The atmosphere must affect opposing players when they arrive. You get the immediate sense of being in a place which is very important. Even though we haven't done so well recently Arsenal is still a great club.

I used to think that Celtic was a *big* club, but my eyes were opened when I came down to London. This is the top club. When people talk about Arsenal they mean the club not the players who have played there. When you talk of Manchester United you are really thinking of the Busby Babes or Denis Law, George Best, Paddy Crerand and all the others. At Arsenal it's not like that. It's an institution. When people talk to me about Arsenal they ask straightaway about the marble halls and so on, just as they ask about the trophy room at the Bernabeu Stadium or the little church that Real have there. There is a tremendous sense of tradition about the place.

When I think about that I find it easier to defend the decision I made. It'll become even easier once we manage to win a trophy or two or get into Europe.

There's no denying I found it hard, and in the early days a lot of that was down to me. The superstar build-up was wrong. It only made life harder. There were times when it damaged me and my agent at that time mishandled my publicity. I've been deeply hurt at times and only two things have helped me through the toughest moments. First, there is my own personality. I can never stay down for long. I have been able to bounce back all my life and I've had to do it during my career with Arsenal more than ever before. Second, there are the Arsenal fans. Without them things would have been a great deal worse. The fans liked me almost from the start; it was as if they took to me, to the way I played and the way I dressed off the field; they seemed to like everything about me. And through the dark days when I've been off form or been dropped from the team or whatever, they have stayed loyal.

The fans, particularly those on the North Bank, kept me going at times. When I felt down they were able to lift me. They have been the club's biggest asset over the past two or three years so far as I'm concerned. People say that fans can make or break you. That's probably right. The way they have stuck by me has been tremendous. I owe them something for their support. There have been times when things weren't going right, when it would have been easy to go in and ask for a transfer. I could have made a case for myself with Don Howe or with the board. But I didn't want to do that because of the way the fans have accepted me. I want to show them what I can do. Perhaps I've managed to do that in little flashes, just enough to keep their interest alive. But that's not enough. I want to show them that kind of football all the time.

Like any supporters at any club, they expect to be entertained. Naturally they like to see their team winning but they also want to see players with individual skills. They want flair added to their football. They're not looking for some kind of soccer stereotype.

When I talk about great players I don't mean people who are strong physically, who can run up and down the park all day. They have their place in the game, but I remember the players with style. I'm sure that the Arsenal fans are the same. They look back to the days of Charlie George, for instance, and maybe they see a little bit of him in me. They appreciate what I'm trying to do, they know from what I've been able to show them that I want to entertain them in every game. I want to play the game the way they want to see it played.

I'm not suggesting that a whole team should be made up of entertainers. In modern football that wouldn't work out. It never did. All good teams have to have a balance. But now the scales have tipped too far the other way. Players are not encouraged to be individualists. It's true not only of Arsenal but of almost all the clubs in the First Division. They don't want entertainers – they want all-purpose functional players. God, it even sounds boring!

There is a lot of talent in the Arsenal team. There is also a huge reservoir of ambition because the players have been hungry for honours for too long. But there are problems at Arsenal which I don't think afflict every club in the country. For some reason or other we are the whipping boys of Fleet Street. Perhaps this is because of the club's image. We are the establishment club, if you like, and so if things go wrong for us it is worse than when things go wrong for a lesser club.

Arsenal players seem to get crucified more often than anyone else. There was an uproar when three of us – Graham Rix, Tony Woodcock and myself – lost our driving licences in less than a year. I'm not going to try to defend us. We were wrong. It was irresponsible. It shouldn't have happened. Unfortunately it did. It also happens to people in different walks of life. It happens to other footballers as well. But when it happened to us it was front-page news or at least big headlines inside the papers. That wasn't how other players at other clubs had their cases dealt with.

I don't know the reason for it. Nor do the other lads. We don't have any doubts, though, that we are the club which gets slaughtered most of all. If a few of us go out together, then there's talk of us drinking too much when we're supposed to be training. When the Spurs lads go out together no one cares. It's got to the stage when the lads don't go out together very often because they don't want the hassle that follows, no matter how quiet the evening might be.

Among footballers the team that has the reputation of being the most social in the world is Liverpool. They go out together and have a few ales or a glass of wine or whatever. Coming back from a game they have a beer or two on the bus and they're always together. Our lads can't do that. I'm not suggesting that the Liverpool players go and get drunk, but they do enjoy themselves. Even Graeme, and Kenny when he was a player, joined in with the rest of them although they were not very keen on going out. But they spent time together and that's a good thing. It builds up team spirit and gives you a chance to sort out any little problems that might come up. It's so much easier to do that socially over a drink than sitting in a dressing room or standing shivering on a training ground. Yet because of the attention focused on Arsenal it's very rare that we get that opportunity. If people would leave us alone it would be so much better. There were times in Glasgow when I thought I lived in a goldfish bowl because punters would come up to me at discos and so on. In London with Arsenal the goldfish bowl is bigger and much more publicized! We can do without that, and I'm sure I'm speaking for all the lads at the club.

This came to a head when the club chairman gave an interview to the *Sun* in which he criticized the players quite strongly. We were angry. All of us were really annoyed about the article and about what the chairman had said because he had never said anything to us. Our view was that he should have spoken to us if he intended to overhaul the disciplinary code at the club, or if he simply wanted to give one or two players a rocket. We would have taken that, of course. So far as losing the driving licences was concerned, we knew that our behaviour had been irresponsible and we deserved to be rapped by the club as well as being dealt with by the courts. But to have it splashed all over the newspaper again when he hadn't even called any of us in to see him – well, we felt that was going too far. Even for the chairman.

Perhaps the chairman thought he had to voice an opinion because there had been adverse stories about the club. Possibly he was trying to counter the bad publicity we had been getting. It hit us totally out of the blue, however, and the day after the article appeared we had a meeting with Don Howe. He knew that none of us was happy about the article and so he called us together to give his view. He told us that the sooner we all forgot about it the better and that it was more important to get on with the job on the field. It was the right thing to say, but the players were hurt.

If I remember rightly, the chairman wasn't too kind to Tommy Caton. As for me, he said that everyone on the North Bank loved me, but some of the people in the stand would disagree with them. That wasn't right because I know that the people in the stand at Highbury have been as good to me as any of the Arsenal fans. It was an unfortunate affair because I'm sure that the chairman did not intend to hurt any of the players at all. The sad thing was that he hurt almost all of us. If he had seen us at Highbury and slammed into us at a meeting we would have found the criticisms a lot easier to take. As it was, while Don told us to forget about it, some of the lads needed time before they could push it to the back of their minds. These are the sort of things that can sour you.

After Stevie Williams joined the club from Southampton another story suggested that he and I were feuding. It was rumoured that Stevie wouldn't pass the ball to me during games, that we didn't speak off the park and that we quarrelled during training. Again it was all rubbish. It's just that 'Nicholas' seems to fit into headlines pretty well. The truth of the situation was considerably different. I first came across Stevie when I was still with Celtic and he was with Southampton – we played against each other in the indoor five-a-side tournament at Wembley. He was a niggly little lad but

I didn't half admire his talent. I respected him from then on. I still do and I'm sure that he feels the same about me. We're on the same wavelength on the field. If I give him the ball and then make space for myself, I'll get it back.

When Stevie arrived at Arsenal it took him some time to settle. One day in the gym I started chirping at him about something, just winding him up a little. It was just a joke so far as I was concerned, but he suddenly kicked the ball at me. At first I couldn't believe it, then I started to laugh and the incident was over. Footballers can be pretty childish at times; we get up to childish pranks and we have childish disagreements which don't last two minutes. That was all it was and yet a story appeared in a Sunday newspaper suggesting that we had had a major row. It was far from the mark and illustrates again, to me, just how much unjustified criticism we often have to take at Highbury.

If we were successful then I'm sure that type of story would be forgotten. Winning games and winning trophies can wipe out bad publicity better than anything else. It could soon be that way with us; when I look at the talent round about me I wonder why it is that we haven't had the success that Liverpool has enjoyed. I didn't know some of the players very well before I moved, even the international players, and perhaps I underestimated their ability at first. Guys like Viv Anderson, Kenny Sansom, Graham Rix, Paul Mariner and Tony Woodcock are class players in any company. It's upsetting when you hear some of them being criticized, because you know what they're like on the park.

Take Viv Anderson, who joined us from Nottingham Forest. He is very talented, great defensively, so much so that very few people can get by him, but I've never seen any defender who looks more like scoring goals. Given a reasonable amount of luck the big man could get himself 15 or 20 goals a season because of the way he comes forward. In set pieces he is very dangerous; he is always looking to get up into the attack and be in on the end of things. There have been times when he has been our best forward. Big Viv has great natural talent. He can look awkward, as though he's all legs, but I don't know any full back in the world who can get goals for his team the way he does.

Until I arrived at Arsenal I was sure that Danny McGrain was the best full back I'd ever seen, certainly the best I'd ever played with. Kenny Sansom is his equivalent in the modern game. Kenny is a complete footballer, just as Danny was in his heyday. He is the ideal full back, good defending, good going forward and always looking comfortable on the ball. It surprises me that I didn't recognize his outstanding talents while I was still at Celtic. Probably it was because I hadn't seen enough of him in action. At the moment I think Kenny Sansom is the best left back in the world. I love Cabrini with Italy but I rate Kenny the world's number one. He's a little lad, around 5 feet 6 inches or so, yet he is quick, and because he is so strong he can get up well. Two good feet and the eagerness to move forward and get himself involved. Kenny has so many good qualities he's frightening.

But the player who surprised me most of all was Graham Rix. When you talk about Rixie then you are talking about sheer class! It's a shame that the fans don't realize this. They always seem to pick on him when we are having a bad time. It's not fair because he is one of the most talented players I've been involved with. His left foot carries more magic than anyone else I've ever played with. When we have the ball we should always be looking to give it to him, and allow him to set up all the moves. Instead, because of the way the game is played in England, Rixie is expected to be chasing back and tackling and defending when he is too good a player for that.

If he had played for Celtic, for example, in a league where players are given more freedom to express themselves, then he would have stood out. He would have been like another Bertie Auld. Bertie had a harder streak than Rixie but Graham has more ability. He loves the game too, loves to work hard, and when things go wrong he tries desperately to put them right. Maybe he tries too hard and that's when the fans get on at him. They're wrong to do that. He is very special. A rare talent and sometimes it seems to be wasted. He should be playing for England all the time. That left foot should be seen in the best of company at the highest of levels!

Then there are Paul Mariner and Tony Woodcock. They are the kind of players you dream about playing with. At Celtic I'd never played alongside a big striker. It was very different when I teamed up with Marrers but he made it easy to play with him. His signing was criticized because he was approaching thirty when he joined us. Perhaps his legs aren't as strong as in his early Ipswich days, but it isn't noticeable. And he still has wonderful positional sense and terrific timing. All that aside, he's great to have around the dressing room. When he arrived – he joined the club after I did – I got on with him straightaway. In those early months at the club I was subdued, still trying to find my feet among the lads; it wasn't natural for me to be like that. But it had been a big change, a major career move, and I was feeling uncertain. But having Marrers around helped me become myself again. He had me chirping and joking in no time at all. Of course, John Wark was his mate down at Portman Road and Marrers likes the Jocks. I think he would like to have been one himself given the chance! As it is, I'm the only Scot at Highbury apart from one young apprentice, and that's unusual for a top club.

Woody is another smashing player. He's the kind of player you can learn from because he has had so much experience: the years at Forest when he was helping them win the European Cup, then the years in the West German Bundesliga with Cologne. Plus his caps with England and his World Cup experience. It's been important for me to have that kind of player beside me.

Why haven't we been more successful? Why, with all that talent around, haven't we reached the full potential

61

of the club and toppled the likes of Liverpool from their spot as top dogs? If we knew the answer we would have done it by now. It's worrying for all of us. If the team playing pattern was adjusted slightly to take more account of the individual styles of the players then it would probably help. If Graham Rix didn't stop to wonder, at times, what he was supposed to be doing inside the team structure and did what comes naturally . . . If I could try some of the things which were so successful for Celtic without worrying about getting a rollicking later if they didn't come off . . . Or if all of us could learn to relax a little more and allow our natural skills full expression . . . There seems to be too much anxiety about the team, too many players – including myself – try too hard at times. When that happens your game can go to pieces.

The fans have been marvellous to me and I'd like them to be the same to all the other lads. Especially Graham Rix. He feels hurt when they get on at him, and he is such a good player. If I were a manager he would be the first name on my team sheet every week – that's how highly I rate him.

Some day the anxiety will go. Some day we will get our act together, and that's when I'll be able to turn to Kenny Dalglish and Graeme Souness and a lot of other people and say to them, 'My choice was right!' The quicker that happens the better!

7

Late Nights with Scotland

One of the greatest disappointments in my career has been the way I slipped out of Scotland's international team.

It was in March 1983 that I gained my first cap for my country and it looked then as if I was going to stay in the side for a long time. And, even better, I was going to be playing alongside Kenny Dalglish. It was the partnership I'd dreamed about, the pairing that the Scots' fans had been waiting to see. For most of that season the fans and the press had been badgering the Scotland manager, the late Jock Stein, to put me into the squad. It was the season following the World Cup in Spain and there was a transition taking place. One or two of the players who had been in the finals of the World Cup were being discarded and other, fresher faces were coming in. The public thought that I should be one of them because that was the season when I was scoring so freely with Celtic.

Three games were played in the European championship between the start of the season and the turn of the year – one of them at Hampden and the other two away from home. The opener was the home game against East Germany. It was the first of our section games in the European championship and was played in the early part of October. By then the calls for my inclusion hadn't developed into the campaign which eventually reached its climax a month or two later. I didn't honestly expect to be selected, so it was no great surprise when the squad was named and I wasn't there. When they won 2–0, with goals from John Wark and Dundee United striker Paul Sturrock, I didn't see a change coming for the next game against Switzerland in Berne a month later.

I was right too and, again, there was no real sense of disappointment. After a victory it would have been most unusual for any manager to start to chop and change his team. Then, on a bleak November night, we crashed to a 2–0 defeat, and even that early in the group games we were under pressure. By then the powerful Belgians had beaten the Swiss 3–0; we were due to travel to Brussels a month later in a bid to keep our hopes alive.

It was then that the clamour for my inclusion grew but Big Jock resisted it. By his reckoning a bad game abroad against Belgium, who had been beaten finalists in the previous European tournament in Italy, might set me back a bit. Probably he was right. In the end we lost that match too, even though Kenny Dalglish scored twice, including what has to be one of the best goals he has scored in his entire career. But when Frank Gray missed a penalty it was too much for the Scots team and even Kenny's inspiration couldn't stop them going down 3–2. It was a great game, but it was still a terrible disappointment and all of us recognized, from that result on, that the jinx which had always struck at our European hopes had arrived again.

So, on to the next match – and this was to be the time for me. Hand-picked by Jock Stein. It all seemed right – a game against Switzerland at home, the promise of a big Hampden crowd behind me, and the fact that a victory might just edge us back into contention for a place in the finals in France the following summer.

Most things worked out according to Jock's script – but the result was wrong. We could only get a draw, 2–2, against a Swiss side which was so much more talented and so much better organized than we had expected. After the first match we knew that they would be hard but we didn't expect them to go forward and score goals in the way they did. Still, I did team up with Kenny and I did get a goal to go with our other one from John Wark. It wasn't enough to give us a win, but it was enough to make me believe that my international career was on a perfect launching pad. Again, though, things failed to go according to plan.

I thought that I was there to stay. So did everyone else. Instead, my Scotland career began to fall apart round about me. There are a lot of reasons for that. Some of the fault is mine, and I accept that. Part is due to the fact that I made the move to Arsenal and the club failed to make any impact in the First Division; with their indifferent form I was forgotten; and part is due to the different circumstances surrounding the World Cup qualifying games. My first big problem with the team came during the transfer negotiations which took me to Arsenal. To be totally honest, the effect of that circus on my Scotland career was disastrous.

The next game I played was against Northern Ireland in the British championship, again at Hampden. Kenny wasn't there. The dream partnership up front had broken up already, and as I write it's never been restored for any length of time. We've started a game together just once and in another game I've come on as a substitute when Kenny was still there on the field. Against the Irish we could only manage a 0–0 draw and I wasn't at my best. The transfer business was getting to me. Also I was asked to play with Andy Gray for the first time. Now Andy is a super player but I'd never played with someone like him before. While we were trying to get something worked out, the Irish defence, solid and reliable as ever with Pat Jennings standing guard behind them, didn't give us a kick.

The next match was at Cardiff and, again, Big Jock elected to rest me. He knew that the biggest game of all for the Scottish supporters was the Wembley game against England. So I watched the Welsh game, saw us win 2–0 at Ninian Park with goals from Andy Gray and Alan Brazil, and then we set up pre-match camp for Wembley at the Moat House Hotel in Harpenden, the headquarters the Scots always use before the match against the English.

That's when things started to go really wrong for me. The Boss expected a lot from me in the game, and playing at Wembley was important for me too. It was my kind of stage; there would be a huge crowd with more than half the 100,000 capacity taken up by the Tartan Army. Apart from that, it's the game that every Scottish schoolboy dreams about playing in. I wasn't any exception. I'd had a good season. More than 50 goals for Celtic, my first Scottish cap and my first international goal to go with it. Now it was to be my first Wembley with Scotland, the biggest and best shop window of them all, as three clubs lined up to buy me for next season.

Everything appeared to be ideal. Until the circus came to town. Then, suddenly, I was being whisked from one meeting place to another for transfer talks when I should have been concentrating on the match itself. Celtic had given the clubs permission to speak to me and Jock Stein couldn't block that. It was an impossible state of affairs for us both.

Looking back, I handled the situation badly. With a bit more experience I would have asked to be left in peace as we prepared for the game. The transfer would still have been on my mind but it would not have taken over in the way it did.

Every time I answered the telephone at the hotel it was someone who wanted to talk about the transfer. Once I went out with Tommy Burns and Roy Aitken for a walk around the village. They were two of my Celtic mates and I wanted to discuss things with them. I needed to talk to somebody about all that was happening to me. So there we were in this quiet little village and they were telling me how great it was that three top clubs were after me, while I was trying to point out to them that I had to make a decision – the right decision. We'd been walking along the road for only ten minutes when a big BMW passed by and there was Ron

Atkinson and Martin Edwards sitting in it wanting to speak to me. That's how it was – I couldn't even have a walk.

All I wanted to do was train and think about the game, and that was impossible. What I should have done was meet the representatives of the three clubs *after* the game against England and then set off for Canada, where I would make up my mind. It was perhaps the one place where I might get enough time to myself to sit down and consider all the points.

The day before the game Jim McLean, the Dundee United manager who was Jock Stein's assistant at that time, came up during training. He drew me aside, asked how I was and then said, 'Is it all getting on top of you, son?'

Now while training I hadn't been thinking about the transfer too much, but away from training, in my room or sitting in the hotel, it was hard to think about anything else. I felt the pressures then and I reckon Jock and Jim had sussed that out for themselves. They'd probably seen little signs that told them things were getting a bit much for me to handle. So Jim said to me, 'Listen, you're going to be picked first for the team, before any of the other forwards who are in the squad. You'll be the one who'll play unless the pressure is getting to you too much. If you feel that, we could just put you on the bench and then bring you on during the game.'

To be fair, maybe I should have said that sitting on the bench would have been best for me, because when it came to the match itself and I went down the tunnel at Wembley for the warm-up I was still thinking about the transfer. There I was heading for the biggest game of my life and all that was going through my mind was the transfer saga: the clubs who were watching me; the meeting that I had coming up. At that point I wished that I had told Jim McLean to leave me out. But at the time he asked me, I thought that would have been taking the easy road. It would have seemed like ducking the issue. I didn't want to back out when the Boss and the fans and everyone else wanted me to play. I felt that I had to do something for them, and what better place to do it than Wembley? Asking to be dropped would have been a cop-out. I would have been letting down too many people and possibly I would have endangered my future international career. After all, I'd only played for Scotland a couple of times, so I was trying to establish myself in the side, and being willing to play always counted in your favour.

The way it turned out I would have been as effective staying on the bench. Or even sitting in the stand. It was all too much for me, and instead of helping Scotland to a win I was taken off in the second half as we slumped to a 2–0 defeat. The English goals came from Bryan Robson and Gordon Cowans. It was a bad night for us.

Going to the bench in the second half while John Wark took over from me remains one of the black spots of my career. What was to have been the realization of all my dreams that season became a nightmare. It was the first time pressure had affected me. Normally I was always able to shrug things off and get on with the game. That June night was so different, so sadly different. I didn't have to be told by anyone how badly I'd flopped. I knew, and I'm still carrying the scars. Some day I want to go back there with Scotland and score a goal which helps beat the English lads. It would give me back some of the self-respect I left behind me on that Wembley pitch.

Within the next week, though, I was off to Canada with the Scotland team. Before our first game in Vancouver I announced I would sign for Arsenal, and with a mind uncluttered by transfer talk and rumours I set out to enjoy the tour games and maybe convince Jock Stein that I could be important to his next World Cup bid. We had two more European ties to play the following season but we knew that we could not qualify there. The Canada tour was designed to prepare a squad for the 1986 World Cup qualifying games.

Some players were missing from the tour because of club calls and Kenny Dalglish was resting after being troubled by injury. But it was a strong enough pool that left London for Vancouver, and the importance of the exercise was underlined by Graeme Souness who left a Liverpool tour in the Far East to join up with us in Canada.

It was a good tour. We won all three games against a Canadian team that was eventually to qualify for the World Cup finals in Mexico. In Vancouver we won 2–0, with goals from the then Aberdeen twosome of Gordon Strachan and Mark McGhee. Then we moved on to Edmonton where we won 3–0. I scored, along with Dundee United's Richard Gough and Graeme Souness. We finished in Toronto, that most Scottish of cities, with another two-goal win. Both were scored by Andy Gray.

By this time I felt I had gone a long way to establishing myself in the team and after the Edmonton game Jock Stein had gone so far as to say, 'That was the real Charlie Nicholas we saw out there. With the transfer business well behind him he was concentrating totally on his game. That's what we want to see from him all the time.'

Unhappily it wasn't to be. I played just one more match for Scotland before a series of problems and the indifferent form of Arsenal saw me banished from the squad. I scored again in that match. It was against Belgium at Hampden as we played out the already lost European group. We drew 1–1 and 23,000 fans saw me equalize in the second half after Belgium had gone in front. The following month we completed that miserable tournament run by going to Leipzig for the return with East Germany. In dreadful conditions of snow and ice we lost again by 2–1. I was out of the side. Kenny joined up with Steve Archibald, and Frank McGarvey came on as substitute.

It was the beginning of the end for me in many ways because my next two appearances for a national side brought with them off-field problems that were to

complicate my situation with Scotland and my relationship with Jock Stein. Indeed, I was caught in the middle
of a row between the Scotland manager and my own
club boss, Don Howe. At the time I had more to worry
me than that. It was the kind of distraction no player
needs and, with my form dipping, Arsenal struggling
and my international career in obvious jeopardy, I could
have well done without it.

It started just under a month later when I was named
in the squad of players for the British championship
game against Northern Ireland in Belfast. Now, as well
as being off form, I was also struggling with an injury
and was forced to pull out of the travelling party. Jock
Stein was told by a 'friend' of mine that I simply hadn't
wanted to go to trouble-torn Belfast. It took a message
from Don Howe to convince him that I was genuinely
injured.

That little bit of bother between the two of them flared
up again when I joined the Under-21 side for their
quarter-final match against Yugoslavia in Belgrade. Jock
had strengthened the side by bringing in full international players like myself to guard the 2–1 lead which
the Under-21 team had gained in the first game at Pittodrie. In the meantime I had been left out of the full side,
which beat Wales at Hampden 2–0, with goals from
Davie Cooper and Mo Johnston, who had moved from
Partick Thistle to Watford a month or two earlier. Still,
the Belgrade trip was a sign that the door had not closed
on me completely and I was determined to take the
opportunity. I knew that a good display – and I was to
play with Mo – would help me back into the full side
for the Hampden game against England which was due
to be played at the end of May. That was my target –
to be back for that one and to get some revenge over the
English lads after my disaster at Wembley.

This time I really brought trouble on myself and the
row with Arsenal that followed didn't help my cause at
all. On the way back from Yugoslavia after the match
I didn't have any illusions that my Scotland career was

coming to an abrupt end! First of all, the night before we were set to fly out from Glasgow, Little Mo, Frank McAvennie and I decided to go out on the town for a few hours. We should have known better, but Mo and I had been away from Glasgow for a while and we wanted to see some of our mates and check out the local scene. It was a mistake, especially with someone as thorough as Big Jock in charge!

Not surprisingly, after the curfew and after we had slipped out through the fire exit, the Big Man had the rooms checked by the trainers. We were missing and so he decided that he would wait for us to come in. We didn't have a chance. He had the hotel staff alerted, and when we tried to slip in through one of the fire doors someone from the hotel staff was waiting. He phoned upstairs, and by the time we came out of the lift the manager was waiting for us. Frank was on another floor but he was caught too and all of us were given a roasting that night. We had another roasting the next morning. Only Mo and I played in the game and I was subbed during the second half when Brian McClair of Celtic took over. We lost in extra time and so we were out of the tournament – and another row blew up as we arrived home.

For quite a spell that season – and it was now March – I'd been playing with damaged ankles. I had a lot of trouble with them and was taking jags and pills in a bid to clear up the injuries. However, the physiotherapist at Highbury had told me that for a proper cure I needed six weeks' rest. My ankles were heavily strapped when I reported for the Scotland Under-21 trip, but because of the row at the time of the Belfast game I decided to report. I told Jock Stein that I had been playing for Arsenal regularly carrying the injuries. But when he took me off during the game I was really bad – I was going about that park like Raymond Burr!

To be fair, I don't think that Don had realized the full extent of the injuries to my ankles. Jock Stein was upset because he was worried about my fitness; he said it was wrong that I should be playing when I was obviously injured. Don took the view that the team needed me; he also stuck up for me at the time. But I realized then that taking pills or getting jags when injured is totally wrong. I'm completely against it now because it's no good for players. A team wants a player fit to play in certain matches, but they don't look far enough into the future to see the possible consequences of someone causing further damage to himself. It's easily done, and almost every player at one time or another has taken some sort of pain killer just so he can play. I don't think I'd ever do it again.

Anyhow, back to my troubles with Scotland. The injury row and the breaking of the curfew definitely saw any hopes of my playing against England at Hampden disappear, although Big Jock did take me to France the following week to play in Marseilles against the team which was to become European champions six weeks later. I was on the bench and came on late in the match, which we lost 2–0 to goals from Giresse and Lacombe.

I was glad that, somehow, I had partially survived the problem because the build-up to the World Cup was on and the qualifying games kicked off the following autumn. I desperately wanted to be a part of them and I knew I had to resurrect my international career to take part. But I knew also that it wasn't going to be easy to get into the team for the opening games against Iceland and Spain at Hampden. Still, I was in the squad when it was named and I played in both matches, although only as a substitute. Even that wasn't too disappointing because in an earlier friendly game against Yugoslavia, which we won 6–1, I scored when I came on. I did the same in the match against Iceland, which we won comfortably by 3–0, with young Paul McStay getting the other goals. Against Spain we scored 3 again, 2 from Mo Johnston and a marvellous goal from Kenny. This time it ended at 3–1, but I didn't get my name on the score sheet.

In Seville for the next match against the Spaniards

we lost 1–0; their centre forward Clos scored a few minutes after half time. Kenny and Steve Nicol took ill on the day of the game and we never managed to look as good as we had at Hampden. Once more I was a substitute and once more I couldn't get the goal we needed.

Our next match was against Wales at Hampden and by this time we all knew that another home win would push us into a commanding position in the group. We flopped that night in front of 62,000 fans, lost to a goal from Ian Rush, and were hammered by the critics and the fans.

What made it worse for me was that again I had blotted my copybook by going out of the hotel and into Glasgow for a couple of drinks. Again Mo Johnston was my companion in crime, but this time we didn't break a curfew. We were out late, too late, but it was several days before the game and neither of us felt that we had done very much wrong. But when the *Evening Times* in Glasgow ran the story you would have thought that we had been responsible for the defeat. Jock Stein covered for us. He refused to confirm that we had been out late and stressed that in any case there had been no curfew in operation so many days before the match. I maintain to this day that if we had won the game against the Welsh we would have heard nothing about the incident. Because we lost, the whole affair became front-page news, with the 'Champagne Charlie' tag hung firmly around my neck again.

That was the last time Jock Stein picked me for any of his squads. Maybe he felt that he had had enough problems from me, although we had a good relationship. I respected him and I know that he liked me and believed in my talent as a player. The times we fell out were caused by childish behaviour on my part. I was either being late or nicking out for a few hours, but I was never out on the eve of a game or even two days before a game.

I think he worried over me because he liked to see

young lads taking care of themselves. He could handle
me because before my time he had handled so many
players who had caused him headaches. I had rows from
him and sometimes I thought he was wrong in the things
he said to me, but I knew, too, that he was concerned
about me, and for me. He was always suspicious of
London and the life down there, which he felt could
spoil a footballer's career.

Yet after that last brush before the Wales game, it
was Jock Stein who got tickets for my Dad and me when
I came up to see Celtic win the Scottish Cup in the
final against Dundee United. He left two complimentary
tickets for us at the front door and I appreciated that
very much. It was as if he was telling me, 'OK, you're
not in the squad right now, but I haven't forgotten you.'
It was the kind of gesture which was so typical of that
man.

8

The Time I Hated Fergie!

Before I left Celtic the traditional soccer rivalries in
Scotland had altered – all because of the rise of the New
Firm of Aberdeen and Dundee United. These two teams
had begun to take over from the Glasgow pair of Celtic
and Rangers – the Old Firm – as the top teams in the
country. Top not in terms of their following, but in terms
of their run of successes at home and in Europe.

In the year or two before my move to Arsenal the
team I had begun to dislike more than any other was
Aberdeen. There was an arrogance about them. And
there was also the fact that at Celtic we found it hard
to beat them. That wasn't easy for us to accept, and our
resentment boiled up into a real dislike and brought
several grudge games between us.

But there were other reasons too. Particularly the
tactics used to stop me. That's why I hated Alex
Ferguson, the Aberdeen manager. After I had been at
Arsenal for a year or so Fergie moved on to the international scene as assistant to Jock Stein for the World
Cup qualifying games. Then, after the tragic death of
Jock at Cardiff, he was appointed Scotland's boss for
the games against Australia and the Mexico finals. By
then I had got to know him a little better, having been
a member of the squad at various times. But until then,
until I met him with Scotland, I really didn't like him.
In fact, if anyone had told me that I would be able to
play under his management I wouldn't have believed
them.

There were one or two really bad incidents involving

Aberdeen and myself and I blamed Fergie for them. At that time the rivalry between the clubs was really strong, and there was at least one clash which became notorious so far as our supporters were concerned. I'm sure that they still talk about it today – it certainly took a long time for me to forget about it. It was a Premier League game up at Pittodrie and in the first few seconds or so Neale Cooper, an old mate of mine from the Scotland Under-18 Youth International team, let me know he was playing. Big Neale flattened me with a crunching tackle before I was out of the centre circle. It happened in another game, and whenever we played Aberdeen I'd find myself man-marked by Neale Cooper. I was convinced then that Fergie had sent the big fellow out to hammer me. My old man couldn't believe that Neale would do that to me. Neale and I had been in the youth team together, and we had got on all right off the park. My Dad wasn't able to come to terms with the fact that the big lad could whack me the way that he did.

It never made any real difference to me so far as Neale was concerned. I used to wind him up a little when we were with the Under-21 team. If we met in the hotel corridor I'd jump back into my room, shouting, 'Look out, big Neale's coming' – things like that. But I didn't bear any grudges towards him. Life is too short in football terms to go through your career harbouring bad feelings against another professional who is trying to do his job.

At that time Big Neale was trying to force his way into the Aberdeen first team. He was the kind of player who would be sent out to do a job by a manager. In this case Alex Ferguson sent him out to man-mark me and on a few occasions, particularly the one I mentioned earlier, I thought he was, to say the least, overzealous in the way he carried out his instructions. I could understand what was going on, but I didn't like it very much.

It was bad enough going to Aberdeen and facing their central defenders Willie Miller and Alex McLeish. They were just becoming dominant then, developing into the partnership which has been at the heart of the Scottish defence for quite some time now. You knew you were going to be in for a hard game if you had to play against them. Having a big powerful lad like Neale Cooper marking you as well didn't make the games against Aberdeen any easier.

It felt as if they were lying in wait for me at Pittodrie. I'd take a look at the match programme in the dressing room before the game. Sure as fate, there would be a piece stressing how dangerous I could be. It would be written by Willie Miller or Alex Ferguson or someone else – but the message which hit me was always the same. I was going to be hammered!

It's little wonder, then, that I grew to hate Fergie. I blamed him entirely though now I know I was wrong. Of course, it was tied up as well with the jealousy all of us at Celtic felt for Aberdeen. The rivalry was so desperate that any little incident was blown up, but the Neale Cooper tackle couldn't be exaggerated. When suddenly you're kicked just after you take the kick-off in a game, you say to yourself, 'What's going on here?' If Willie Miller whacks you in the first minute as you're going for a ball which has been played up to you, that may be acceptable. It seemed to me this was out of order.

I'm used to the game being physical, especially in Scotland. The defenders were allowed to get away with much more than in England when I first came to Arsenal. When I arrived at Highbury the tackle from behind had been outlawed by the referees, but that ruling had not been adopted north of the Border. Up there they could whack you from behind for the full ninety minutes and get away with it. You learned to accept the knocks. You didn't like it, but you had to learn how hard life can be at the top.

I was given a lesson in that when I was just sixteen years old. The two strikers in possession of the first team places at Celtic Park were Frank McGarvey and George McCluskey. One day I was called over by manager Billy

McNeill to join the first-team training at Barrowfield. They had an exercise worked out in which the midfield player pushed the ball up to the strikers, who were being tightly marked by the two central defenders. The object was for the striker to get the ball back, allowing the midfield man to come up in support and possibly get in a shot at goal.

I'd seen the lads working out from the other end of the training ground where the reserves and the ground-staff lads did their work, so I knew what was wanted. But I didn't realize how hard Billy made it for the strikers. For two weeks he had me taking part in this particular exercise. And for those two weeks big Roddy McDonald, who is now with Hearts, tackled me from behind. Every time the ball reached me, *whack*! I was up in the air, then someone like Danny McGrain was picking me up off the ground and telling me not to worry. I couldn't say anything, either. This was the first real chance I had been given to train with the full squad and so I had to bite my tongue and carry on with the training I was given. God, I was sore. I doubt if I've ever been kicked with such consistency in all my career. I took terrible stick and all the players felt sorry for me – I felt sorry for myself.

Later on I clocked what was happening. Billy was telling big Roddy to give me a kick. He wanted to give me a hard time in training because it would prepare me for what I would have to face when I played in the Premier League. It was shrewd thinking because it taught me to take my lumps without retaliating or squealing too much. It's just part of a striker's life. All of us have to accept it at one time or another; it's just that some of us get it that bit harder. And we're not always equipped to do very much about it. Certainly there was no way that I would ever have been able to take on Neale Cooper even though I might have felt like it at the time. Even my 'commando' training from Billy McNeill and Roddy McDonald hadn't prepared me for that Aberdeen treatment!

It's easier now, looking back at the situation, to understand the bad blood that grew between the two teams. It had also happened between Rangers and Aberdeen for a spell – and has happened since, too – and I believe that it has come about for the same reasons. Aberdeen, and to a lesser extent Dundee United, are taking over from the Glasgow clubs as the most successful teams in Scotland. The Old Firm don't like it, the Old Firm players don't like it and the Old Firm fans don't like it.

From a player's point of view I must admit that I disliked the streak of arrogance which Aberdeen brought onto the field with them. As a youngster in Glasgow I'd grown up a Celtic supporter, and in following Celtic you also learned to hate Rangers. When I first played against them I used to look at them coming onto the field and all the childhood feelings used to rise again. Yet at the time I never knew any friction between the teams on the park. You'd have a niggle or two, but you wouldn't find any really serious trouble affecting the games.

I remember being bitterly disappointed in my first Old Firm game at Ibrox when we lost 3–0. I was taken off because Derek Johnstone marked me out of the game. Beforehand I had reckoned that I could take him because he was overweight and had slowed down a lot, but he had a lot of experience behind him and during the game he'd be grabbing my jersey or giving me a little nudge or hitting me from behind. But there was nothing really nasty about it. What happened in that game was what happened week after week in other games we played in the Premier League, the kind of things you expect and accept.

But against Aberdeen some things were unacceptable at times. The Neale Cooper tackles, for example. Yet even without them I think we would have reacted badly to Aberdeen because we were going into games knowing that we might be beaten. Indeed, it would be more honest to say that we were expecting to be beaten more often than not. They seemed to have the Indian sign on us and we didn't take kindly to it at all. They had good players and so did we. But tactically they were ahead of us. They were better organized and more patient, while, as always at Celtic, we went out to attack in every game. Aberdeen simply waited for us, and then, when we had exposed our defence, hit us on the break. They were deadly. They were successful. They were arrogant. And we couldn't accept that.

It was only when I left Celtic after my transfer to Arsenal that I realized how short-sighted our outlook was. In fact, even before the move, once I had made up my mind to leave Scotland, the parochial view I held began to disappear. For instance, when Aberdeen went to Gothenburg and beat Real Madrid in the final of the European Cup Winners' Cup, I felt really pleased for them. Obviously it was something I would have liked to have done with Celtic, but I was delighted that a Scottish team had been able to win another European trophy, following Celtic's Lisbon victory in the European Cup in 1967 and Rangers' success in the Cup Winners' Cup in Barcelona in 1972. Keeping Scotland's name going in Europe was important, and it was right that it should be Aberdeen who won the cup that night. Their victory was the biggest boost the game in Scotland had had in more than ten years. Dundee United also deserved success because in the eighties they have done more to keep up the reputation of Scottish clubs on the Continent than either of the two Glasgow giants!

Aberdeen at that time had a very balanced side. Wee Gordon Strachan would make all sorts of fancy moves; he could cause any defence in the world problems when he was on song. On the other side Peter Weir created the same kind of openings as Gordon did. Up front their main striker was Mark McGhee. And these three were allowed to get on with the job because there were other players on the team organizing different aspects of the game. At the back was Willie Miller controlling the defence, and in midfield Neil Simpson would work for the full ninety minutes, making sure that area was kept solid like every other part of the team. It was that sort

Above: Charlie is challenged by Chris Hughton and Ossie Ardiles during a London derby with Spurs

Below left: A tense moment as Charlie joins a defensive wall in a New Year's day game against Spurs

Below right: The sight that the North Bank love to see – a jubilant Charlie after scoring a goal

Above: The disappointing game at Wembley.
Here Charlie faces up to a challenge from Terry Butcher while Gary Mabbutt looks on
Below left: Charlie with his idol Kenny Dalglish as the pair enjoy a break from
training with the Scotland squad
Below right: Charlie in World Cup action for Scotland against Iceland at
Hampden Park. Here he sends a shot for goal as an Icelandic player tries
unsuccessfully to block the ball

Above left: The Scotland squad at work with the late Jock Stein directing operations. His assistant Jim McLean stands behind Charlie

Above right: Aberdeen manager Alex Ferguson – the man Charlie once 'hated' but now likes and respects – took over as Scotland World Cup boss after the tragic death of Jock Stein

Below: Pat Jennings, one of Charlie's heroes, stops him with this brave save in a game against Northern Ireland at Hampden

Some of the troubles which haunt strikers in the English first division, as a defender literally gets to grips with Charlie

of balance and organization that we couldn't match. We were too keen to have a go, just get on with the game and chase goals and try to entertain the fans. Even when we lost matches we looked entertaining – but you don't win cups and leagues by attacking all the time. Every other aspect of the game has to be as well organized and as well worked out as the forward play. If you don't do that then you will run into trouble, particularly when you go into Europe. It's no use trying to play there using the same techniques which can bring success at home in Scotland. In Europe it doesn't work so often. Just as it wouldn't work in the English First Division.

Recently there has been a lot of speculation about British cups and British leagues and I've been asked how the top Scottish teams would perform against the First Division sides down here. I'd say that Aberdeen and Dundee United would do better than Celtic or Rangers because they are the two teams which are best organized in the Premier League. They learned the principles of the modern game early on in the Top Ten set-up. It's the way they have adapted which has made them so successful in the past few years.

I enjoyed playing in the Premier League. It didn't bother me that we had to play the same teams at least four times every season. In fact, I would have preferred to have played Aberdeen or Rangers or Dundee United more often rather than play one of the lesser teams. I felt that it increased the professionalism in the game in Scotland and it certainly led to the growth in the power of Aberdeen and Dundee United. They thrived on the atmosphere; they perfected their set-ups and, with increased revenue from their homes gates, they were able to hold on to their star players much more easily than before. Under freedom of contract, of course, there were still players who would move. But no longer did these two clubs have to sell to survive financially.

When I was a kid teams would come to Celtic Park and be beaten by 6 or 7 goals. The Premier League changed all that. Now there are maybe half a dozen teams who are able to challenge. In the old days Celtic and Rangers fought it out at the top almost every season. That doesn't happen so often now because there are not so many poor teams. OK, every season perhaps one team becomes detached early on and look candidates for relegation even before Christmas comes along. But, in general, the standard of the game has risen and Aberdeen and Dundee United have benefited more than the Old Firm.

Celtic and Rangers wouldn't do particularly well in a set-up which included the top English teams. At the moment Rangers don't have enough good players, and I'm afraid that what I know about the present Celtic team suggests that the club still has not learned how teams should be organized for the modern-day game. Celtic are rather like Spurs. They look tremendous one week and then dreadful the next because essentially they play off the cuff, trying to attack and entertain and keep up the cavalier attitude to the game for which they have always had a reputation down the years. When it comes off it's marvellous. I know because I took part in some great games when everyone was on song and everything went right. On those days the football could be sparkling.

The other side of the coin is that when a few players are off form the whole thing can collapse. It's almost as if the club has refused to move with the times. You can respect them for that in some ways – but to be a successful club regularly at a level higher than the Premier League in Scotland, requires a different attitude. If they went into a British league without changing they would sit around the middle of the table and probably never qualify for Europe – the place where really *big* clubs have to play their football! Dundee United would do better in a British league because they have a good basic set-up and good players inside the team pattern. Whether they have the strength in depth to compete week after week at a higher level than they are at the moment is another matter.

Aberdeen are different again. They have a strong squad of players plus the proper organizational skills to adapt to playing in a different environment. They also have Alex Ferguson as their manager. That alone should guarantee them some kind of success in an all-British set-up. There is no way that they would be winning leagues or cups automatically season after season but they would be in with a shout for whatever honours were available.

It must seem funny that the guy I hated for so long when I was with Celtic should suddenly be getting praise. It's not because he is in charge of the World Cup squad; but since his involvement with Scotland I've got to know Fergie a lot better and I have acquired a tremendous respect for the man and the way he approaches the game. As a player with the squad I felt as comfortable with him when he was assistant to Jock Stein as I felt with Jock himself. I was totally impressed by Alex Ferguson from the moment he joined the squad, which was for the friendly game against Yugoslavia in the build-up to the World Cup qualifying matches. His knowledge of the game struck me more than anything else about him. On the personal level I have found it impossible not to like Fergie. And as for his handling of players, I have come to admire him greatly. I never doubted his ability as a manager because Aberdeen beat Celtic too many times to allow me to underestimate him.

Before Fergie took over as the Scotland assistant manager, his north-east rival Jim McLean had the job. He is a great coach and a great manager, but he was different in his approach. He didn't smile a lot and it was hard to crack a joke with him. Fergie joins in the fun. He jokes with players, kids them; Jim seemed to worry much more. Fergie is very thorough in his preparations, and the way he talks before a game shows how deeply he studies football and the players he is involved with.

I'm not alone in changing my mind about Fergie. After some comments he made a few years ago about 'highly paid Anglo-Scots', Graeme Souness, his World Cup skipper for Mexico, wasn't too keen on him either. But they made their peace the first day Fergie moved to Scotland as assistant manager. And after the tragedy in Cardiff, Graeme went on record as stating that Fergie was the man that the Scottish Football Association should appoint to guide the team to the finals for the fourth successive time. Graeme recognized Fergie's ability, appreciated his knowledge of the game, and knew how well he had established himself with the pool of players. It is not easy to be accepted by an international squad – Fergie gained acceptance almost immediately. And while Graeme's voice, as captain of the team, carried more weight than any of the others, it was significant that Kenny Dalglish, too, wanted Fergie to take the job and fully backed his appointment when it was announced. I doubt if there was one player in the squad who would have gone against him. Basically he is the kind of manager players are happy to follow. Yet there is a steeliness about him, too, which means that no one ever tries to step out of line.

After I had been left out of his first two squads he took the trouble to speak to me about my own position regarding the Mexico finals. I went up to play in a testimonial match for the Aberdeen defender John McMaster, who had been forced out of the game because of injury. My old manager Billy McNeill was in charge of the team which I played in. Afterwards, Fergie told me that he thought I had the talent and skills that the Scotland team would need in Mexico, and laid down the gauntlet for me. It was up to me, he stressed, to get my act together and to show enough in my club games with Arsenal to force my way back into his plans. He didn't have to do that. But he went out of his way to encourage me, to give me the boost that perhaps I needed at that time. It was important to me and underlined, again, just how much the personal touch can mean between a player and a manager.

I don't often misjudge people. In fact, I pride myself

on being able to size a person up quickly, and my early impressions aren't usually wrong. But so far as Alex Ferguson is concerned, I was way off line back in those early days when I was making my name with Celtic!

9

Beckenbauer, Cruyff and Europe

The two things I've missed more than anything else since my transfer from Celtic to Arsenal are the success that I knew with Celtic, when I helped them win two Scottish Premier League titles and a League Cup, and playing in Europe, something that Celtic did every single season. Sure, I've played in Europe with Arsenal in pre-season tournaments or friendly games but not in the real nitty-gritty atmosphere of one of the three major European competitions. With Celtic I played in two of the three European competitions – the Champion's Cup, the blue riband of tournaments, and the Cup Winners' Cup.

Unfortunately we didn't get very far in either competition, but I was left with indelible memories of the games we played. I was also left with the very strong belief that travelling abroad to these competitive matches and also touring before the season starts help to build understanding in a team. Off the park morale is often better when everyone is mixing and living together for some length of time. And on the field you learn how team-mates will respond to certain situations much better than you can at home. Don't ask me why, because I'm not sure I can give you the answer. Perhaps it's just that in the time you spend together the major topic of conversation is the game and how you will play, and all the talking creates a better understanding among the players. That was the case in my third season with

Arsenal. We took a break at the start of December and went to Trinidad for close on a week. We came back, lost our first game, but then went on to beat Liverpool and Manchester United to hoist ourselves towards the top of the table after an indifferent run. I'm sure that the boost in our form came from the week the lads had spent together.

In Europe with Celtic we had good times and bad times. But I always felt that we were learning a little more about the game. One of the first lessons I learned came from our manager Billy McNeill when we went to West Germany to play a friendly against Hamburg in the Volkspark Stadion. The match was to be a warm-up before we went on to Holland to take part in the prestigious Feyenoord tournament in Rotterdam, along with hosts Feyenoord, the Belgian side Anderlecht, and the Czechs from Dukla Prague. The Hamburg game wasn't so much a warm-up as a lesson for all of us, particularly yours truly, a lesson that was hammered home to me by Big Billy before we reached Rotterdam.

Hamburg were a strong side with a scattering of West German international players, including Felix Magath and Manny Kaltz. But the one player I saw was Franz Beckenbauer, the Kaiser himself, back from his spell with New York Cosmos and now guiding Hamburg and helping the fans forget Kevin Keegan, who had returned to English football with Southampton. By this time, the summer of 1981, I'd played three matches in a European competition and they were in the Cup Winners' Cup the previous season. But this was the first time I'd encountered one of the game's giants. It's too simple to say I was overawed – it was more than that. Here was a player I'd been watching on the telly for years. Ever since I was a kid he had been dominating European football. He had won the European Cup and the Cup Winners' Cup with Bayern Munich. And he had captained West Germany to their World Cup victory in 1974. It was hard to believe that I was on the same pitch as he was.

I was so awestruck I could hardly play. I was

wandering around like a little boy lost. He was the first legendary player I'd ever come up against in my career. There was I, just nineteen years old, and Beckenbauer was marking me. I didn't kick a ball all night. All I did was watch how he played. If the ball was passed to me I would simply play it off to Davie Provan or someone else. I didn't really want the ball. I just wanted Beckenbauer to get it. If I had had my way I would have passed the ball to Franz Beckenbauer because I could have watched him all night. It was a thrill to be able to see him in action at close quarters.

However, I wasn't able to watch him for the full ninety minutes. Billy McNeill took me off in the second half and told me then something that I've never, ever forgotten. He took me aside and said, 'You have to learn that when you play against these players with huge reputations you simply have to go out and beat them. That is the only way you will gain respect from them because that is how they have earned their reputations.' It was absolutely true and a lesson I took to heart. But I'll never, ever forget that night. I hung around that park like a spectator. It's a wonder I didn't take an autograph book on with me and say to Beckenbauer, 'Just sign here, please, Franz.' But after the warning from Billy McNeill I've tried not to let myself be so overawed again. Now, five years on, it sounds a bit daft, but that night there was nothing I could have done to alter how I felt.

My earlier excursions into Europe the previous season (1980–81) had taught me how to deal with certain problems. At least they had prepared me for some of the difficulties teams get into when they play on the Continent. We played against two teams that were almost unknown. They came from behind the Iron Curtain, which meant we had to travel across Europe, a journey that no British team ever relishes. When you go into Eastern Europe you face long flights, poor hotel accommodation and poor food.

The season before, in 1980, I'd travelled with the team

to Madrid. I was a youngster learning the ropes and visiting the magnificent Bernabeu Stadium for the first time. I'd been taken along to learn a little about Europe – just to be in a stadium with a huge crowd was something special for me. I was the seventeenth man that night when we lost 3–0 to Real Madrid in the Spanish capital after winning 2–0 at Celtic Park. It was a major disappointment for the club because a win would have carried us into the semifinals. Still, it was an experience to remember, but it bore no resemblance to Miskolc in Hungary or Timisoara in the wilds of Rumania. Although Europe was so important in teaching me my trade as a footballer, it also provided several major blows – and the 1980–81 season brought the worst of them all from Politechnica Timisoara. Now there's a name to conjure with: I'd never heard of them before and I've never heard of them since. In fact, I wish that I'd never heard of them at all!

That was the first season in which I broke into the first team after a reserve year which had seen me score 25 goals in 37 games. Barring my way to regular first-team football were George McCluskey and Frank McGarvey, who had joined the club from Liverpool the previous season for a record Celtic fee. And in the first European game, a preliminary-round clash in the Cup Winners' Cup against the Hungarians, Diosgyoeri Miskolc, they spelled out how difficult any breakthrough would be. By half time, as torrential rain poured down on the park, the 28,000 fans had not seen the scoring feats they wanted, but what a change after the interval. Frank helped himself to a hat trick in his first European game. George added two more and Dom Sullivan another to give the team a 6–0 win and a certain passport into the first round proper of the tournament.

I got my chance to play in a European competition in the second-leg game – and I scored too, after twenty-four minutes. But it didn't herald another feast of goals. Instead we allowed the Hungarians to come back into the game and ended up losing 2–1 in a match we should have won if we had taken all our chances. Still, an aggregate 7–2 win was something to be pleased about. The following weekend I stayed in the team and in my first full Premier League game scored 2 goals against Partick Thistle, who had Alan Rough in goal! I was also named in the Scotland Under-21 squad for a match in Sweden. It was a memorable week for me, and I thought that I would continue playing in Europe as a regular member of the side.

That's how things worked out. When the draw was made we were given another Iron Curtain trip and that's when I met up with Politechnica Timisoara for the first and, I hope, the last time! There were 30,000 fans at Celtic Park that night, all hoping that we would hammer in another 6 goals or at least enough to carry us into the next round. We started as if we were going to give ourselves a comfortable lead for the difficult return leg and I scored 2 goals in the first half. The first one arrived after only eighteen minutes: their goalkeeper dropped a cross by Davie Provan at my feet and I was able to send it into the net. Then, a few minutes before half time, I scored with a header. The supporters waited for the rest of the goals to follow. Unfortunately that wasn't the way the script went for us after half time. Tommy Burns hit the bar with a marvellous shot but it was the Rumanians who grabbed a goal in the seventy-eighth minute. Afterwards Billy McNeill admitted, 'The players have left themselves a difficult task in the return – but we are good enough to win.'

We were too. But we lost, and that result brought another important lesson in my European schooling, another I won't forget in a hurry. The Greek referee taught me that you must always expect the worst when you go to some of these remote European venues. I will never forget the guy who marked me in the game – and I mean marked me! He was called Sunda; he was a great big, rough fellow, a proper villain, about ten years older than me. He kept pulling my hair and poking me in the eye. I was just eighteen and this was the first time I'd come up against anything as vicious and as blatant as this. Looking to the Greek referee for protection was a waste of time. Everything went the Rumanians' way from the moment Danny McGrain won the toss. He chose the way he wanted to play and was not allowed to do so. You didn't have to be very intelligent to realize that things were going to be stacked against you after an opener like that!

In the opening quarter of an hour the referee made it totally clear that we were in trouble. He booked three of our players – Tom McAdam, Peter Latchford and Murdo MacLeod. A few minutes later he sent off Roddy McDonald along with one of the Rumanian players. We knew that to lose just one goal would be enough to send us tumbling out of the tournament because of the away goal the Rumanians had snatched in Glasgow. With three players booked and every decision going against us, it was incredibly difficult, but we should have managed to hold out. That we didn't is down to the referee again. Our goalkeeper, big Peter Latchford, was barged in the back when he rose to hold a free kick towards the end of the game. He dropped the ball and they scored the single goal they needed.

The Rumanians had a band playing all through the game, blasting out their club song, which was the same tune as 'Yellow Submarine'. The club complained but no one did anything to stop it although it was against UEFA rules.

The game was a disaster for us and a personal low point for me because that was the first time I'd known the despair of losing in a European tie. I took it very badly. I still remember weeping in the hotel after the game, reacting to the combination of all that had happened to us – the biased refereeing, the personal abuse I'd had handed out to me and the fact that Timisoara were a bad team. Honestly, they were rubbish. With any kind of luck in our finishing in the first leg we would have scored 5 or 6 against them, and no matter what dirty tricks they got up to in the return they wouldn't have been able to beat us. All of us had set our hearts on having a long run in Europe and here we were, out after just two games. We were out, really, in the first round, because the game against the Hungarians had been an extra, preliminary-round, tie. It was a terrible night in a terrible place and even though my own form remained good – I was scoring regularly in the Premier League by now – it was hard to accept that such a bad side had been able to beat us.

The next round saw them knocked out of the competition by the English First Division team West Ham. The Hammers did what we should have done. They scored 4 goals against them at Upton Park. That 4–0 win set them up for the second leg in Rumania. While the Hammers lost by the same 1–0 score as we did – and probably had a similarly bad experience – they coasted through to the quarter finals. They lost there to the Russian team Dinamo Tbilisi, who went on to take the trophy. All of us at Celtic Park, though, looked on that season in Europe as a lost opportunity.

The same couldn't be said about the next attempt we had. This time we went into the European Cup as Scottish champions. We were drawn to face the full might of Juventus in the opening round of the competition. It was hard to believe that we could draw such famous opponents in the first round when traditionally teams with sizable reputations in Europe can look forward to a relatively easy passage.

Still, we were reasonably well prepared for the clash with the Italian champions. We had had the game in Hamburg and we had won the Rotterdam tournament. We had knocked out the host club Feyenoord in the first match and then gone on to another win over Dukla, the Czech Army side from Prague, in the final. It was a boost for the players and for the thousands of Celtic fans who had flocked to the Dutch city for the game. These fans created a tremendous atmosphere and helped us to our wins. Murdo MacLeod was the man who found the killer touch against the Czechs with 2 goals in the first twenty minutes and they were enough to see us through to a 2–0 win – an important win for the sake of our confidence.

However, we knew that Juventus would be formidable opposition, probably the most formidable on the whole of the Continent. They had just won the Italian championship for a record nineteenth time. They had half a dozen players who were in the Italian World Cup squad – the same squad who were to win the Jules Rimet trophy in Spain the following summer, less than a year after we met them. Still, Juventus, with the likes of Tardelli, Zoff, Bettega, Cabrini, Scirea and even Liam Brady, weren't going to dazzle me. Billy McNeill's advice had got the hero-worshipping out of my system.

We played quite well in the first leg at Celtic Park with 60,000 fans watching. You never get many chances against the Italians and this was no exception. They played very tight, just as we had expected, but we still managed to break them down and get one goal. I thought we did quite well.

I had been dropped from the team before the match and was playing, I think, because Frank McGarvey was injured. I was still only nineteen and was marked that night by Claudio Gentile, one of the most feared defenders in the world. He had a formidable reputation and I knew that I mustn't allow myself to be dominated in the way I had at Hamburg. That was very much in my mind as we warmed up for the game; it was going to be a test in more ways than one. As it turned out, Gentile was the hardest player I have ever played against in my life. He would do anything to upset me. He nipped me, he pulled my hair, he held my jersey – all the annoying, niggly things that referees don't always pick up on; even the fans can't see what's going on. But they are enough to distract you or hold you back or simply keep you on edge wondering what the hell he's going to do next. Who would imagine that a defender would nip your backside during a game? That was the way he carried on. Gentile had it down to a fine art – he'd catch you when you least expected it. He was able to stop you in your tracks when you were ready to make a run by grabbing you. He was seldom caught at it because he was so clever. I managed to hold my own against him, but it was a hard match. I've never come up against anyone else who has the dirty tricks off to such perfection.

The second leg was something else. The Stadio Communale in Turin where Juventus play their home games must be one of the most intimidating grounds in the whole world of football. I'd put it alongside the stadium in Seville where Scotland met Spain for the World Cup qualifying match. As we went onto the pitch about an hour before the kick-off to get the feel of things, we found ourselves the target for oranges and potatoes, a whole variety of missiles. What a welcome that was. We hadn't even done anything then. OK, we'd scored at Celtic Park and arrived at their stadium with a one-goal lead, but there hadn't been any trouble off the field. The game at Celtic Park had taken place without any bother. Yet we were villains to those crazy fans. Believe me, they were crazy. During the game there were times when they seemed to go beserk for no reason at all. There would be a period of calm, then they would go mad again. It's a frightening atmosphere for a visiting team.

We had already suffered a bad blow before the game when Danny McGrain was ruled out because of a hair-line fracture; Davie Moyes took his place. Davie did well, but the experience of someone like Danny is vital in that kind of situation and we missed him. Frank McGarvey had recovered from his injury and he and George McCluskey were back together again. I was one of the substitutes.

We lost 2–0 that night. Juventus' first goal came after about half an hour, when Roy Aitken sliced a free kick and Virdis picked up the ball and raced through on his own to smash a shot past Pat Bonner. Then, not too long before the interval, Roberto Bettega got the other.

We tried to get back into the game, and at least Dino Zoff knew he had been playing when he was tested a few times, but the task would have been beyond most teams by the time Juventus were two goals in front. We knew that one goal would carry us through, but we couldn't get it. Liam Brady had a magnificent night for Juventus before he was taken off near the end.

To round off a miserable night for Celtic, hundreds of our supporters who had travelled to back the team were attacked by Juventus fans in the streets of Turin. Buses were stoned and four Celtic fans were stabbed and ended up in hospital. After the 'welcome' we had received in the ground none of us was surprised when we heard what had happened. It was an ugly side to the game and should never have happened; despite my little problems with Gentile, the games had been good. Juventus had been entertaining and there was no bad blood between the players. Just a few broken hearts on our side again.

For me the season went into a decline. After the sparkling start to my first-team career with Celtic, things somehow ground to a halt so far as I was concerned. If not exactly a halt, it was a period when I made hardly any progress. I played mainly in the reserves as Frank McGarvey and George McCluskey had teamed up again as the main strikers. Yet the previous season (1980–81) could scarcely have been better. From the time I was introduced early on in the year everything went right. I made forty-one first-team appearances and I scored 28 goals, just one behind Frank. It was especially good because I managed to score in all four competitions that we took part in: the Premier League, which we won, the Scottish Cup and the League Cup, where we reached the semi-finals, and the European Cup Winners' Cup.

It was then that I learned how hard it is, at times, to sustain form. To complete a nightmare period, I broke my leg in the reserve game at Morton and had to sit out most of the rest of that season. Still, the team were able to clinch the title once again and the following season, restored to the first team, I was back in European Cup action. Once more we had a tremendously difficult first-round tie – against the Dutch side Ajax of Amsterdam who had been inspired to their title win by the return of their most famous player, Johan Cruyff. Again my mind flashed back to Beckenbauer, and this time the comparison was a great deal more obvious than it had been for the Juventus game.

Here was Cruyff back in Holland after spells in the States – just like Kaiser Franz had been when I encountered him in West Germany. And, again, Cruyff was a player who had been one of my heroes when I was a youngster watching the superb Dutch side on the telly. OK, he was a veteran, but someone with special skills, someone who belonged in any gallery of greats, in any soccer Hall of Fame that you care to draw up. He said some nice things about me before the first game at Celtic Park and it made me all the more determined to do well. We felt that we could win, that maybe, just maybe, this was to be the chance of European glory that we had all been chasing so desperately over the past few seasons.

Almost 60,000 turned up at Celtic Park to see the game and to take their first look at the emerging Danish talents who were to loom so large in every Scottish mind during the run-up to the World Cup finals in Mexico. Little Jesper Olsen was there and his fellow countrymen Soren Lerby and Jan Molby, who is now with Liverpool. Olsen scored that night and so did Lerby. Olsen is now with Manchester United and Lerby with Bayern Munich, and their performances with Ajax and with Denmark against England in the European Championships helped to put them there. This was the first time we had encountered them and their exciting talents and they held us to a draw in the first leg.

I scored that night with a penalty, and our other goal came from Frank McGarvey. We did well and should have won, but Ajax were talented and Cruyff pulled all the strings. He was magnificent, but I remembered Hamburg and Big Billy's little chat, so didn't let his presence on the field overshadow everything else. Still, I couldn't help but admire the way he controlled the team. Every little thing they did seemed to be influenced by him. His passing and his positional sense were unimpaired and the way he talked to the younger lads round about him was obviously very important to them both as individuals and in their team performance. With the 2–2 score line the Dutch went home happy, but the great man left Glasgow saying kind things about me, which was nice.

I made up my mind that I wanted to impress him just as much, if not more, in the return. The odds looked to be stacked against us when we arrived in Amsterdam and the word from the Ajax camp at the seaside resort of Schevingen was that they were confident of going through. Like ourselves, they were a team who had won the tournament before, and then, after the great days of Cruyff and Neeskens and the rest, they had faded from their former top position in Holland and Europe. This, they were sure, was the year they would head back to greatness. By getting a draw at Celtic Park they had convinced themselves and their fans that this would happen. Of course, we were equally determined that it wouldn't happen. We knew that to have any chance of going through we would have to score because, with away goals counting double in the event of a draw, the Dutch were already beating us. But we also realized that we would have to curb the very special skills of Cruyff. That job was handed to Graeme Sinclair and he did it magnificently that night in the Olympic Stadium, where a crowd of 60,000 had turned up to watch the clash. We scored first and I was the scorer. It was a goal that I still savour. Any striker will tell you the same. When you get a goal which is a little bit special you really enjoy it; it's even better when you score in an important game in one of football's most famous stadiums in front of a big crowd.

The goal gave our supporters – and we had brought several thousand with us – the lift they wanted. Suddenly

97

they sensed that we could still go through, and although Ajax equalized through Vanenberg we still looked the better team. In the dying minutes we proved it – the goal we needed to win that game and to take us into the second round came through George McCluskey. It was one of the club's most famous victories and all of us recognized that. There is a tremendous feeling when you win away from home in a European tie. This time it was heightened because we had beaten a top team.

We headed back to our hotel for a champagne celebration and on the way I sat very quietly in the back of the team bus biting my tongue to avoid what could have been my most embarrassing moment. It had been my ambition to get Cruyff's shirt. We had not been able to swap jerseys on the field – he had been substituted ten minutes from the end of the game – so I went to the Ajax dressing room afterwards to ask for the jersey. At first I couldn't get in. The door was shut and they were getting a bit of stick from their coach, probably because we had just beaten them. Anyhow I waited a little, and then tried again. When I got in Cruyff was sitting on the treatment table. I asked him if we could change jerseys. He bent down and picked up an Ajax jersey from one of the bins and handed it to me.

I couldn't believe that it had been so easy. There I was with the great man's number fourteen jersey – Cruyff always played with fourteen on his shirt whether with Ajax or Holland. I didn't look at it. I just took it, stuffed it into my hold-all and thanked him, feeling that this was a real night to remember. He took my jersey, and I went out and got on the bus feeling well pleased with life. I didn't say anything to any of the other players. I had decided that I'd wait to get back to the hotel and then spring it on them. But there we were on the bus and George McCluskey said, 'Well, I got it this time, lads. I got Johan's top.' Sure enough, he produced the number fourteen. I sat there saying nothing and wondering which jersey I had. When I got to my room I found out I had number twenty-three. I've never been so choked in my life. I didn't tell anyone. Cruyff had just leaned over and handed me any old Ajax strip – I still don't know whose jersey it was. To be honest, I don't care a lot either!

We were into the next round, and this time, true to form, we picked another top side. The Spanish champions Real Sociedad who came from San Sebastian in the Basque country in the north of Spain. They were a powerful team with the veteran Spanish keeper Arconado and internationals Ufarte, Satrustegui, Uralde and Zamora. All of them had played in the World Cup finals the previous summer and two of them were to score the goals that put us out of the competition. We lost 2–0 in the first leg in Spain and were disappointing. We didn't play as well as we could and Satrustegui and Uralde got a goal each. Murdo MacLeod scored twice in the return leg for us, but again Uralde stepped in to score, an important goal for them, and we went out on a 3–2 aggregate. It was so disappointing, and a stark contrast to the champagne of Amsterdam. We felt it even more because we had tasted that little bit of success in the Olympic Stadium. We had thought that we were on our way to fresh glory in Europe, but the dream didn't last very long.

However, we felt that we still had the potential for success among the top clubs on the Continent. In the Sociedad tie there had been almost 55,000 people at Celtic Park and nearly 60,000 saw Ajax. That was proof that the crowd potential was there, and although we had been out of touch in Spain we all felt that, given a break or two – or the easy draw we always seemed to miss – we might have gone considerably further in the tournament. The Spaniards went on to beat Sporting Lisbon in Portugal in the quarter finals before losing to Hamburg by the odd goal in the semifinals. The West Germans took the trophy, beating Juventus 1–0 in the final in Athens. Against that kind of background it was clear that Celtic were heading in the right direction. But, of course, that was to be my last game in Europe for Celtic.

99

The following close season my contract ended and I was on my way to Arsenal.

Before going, however, I won another medal with the club and helped them to win the League Cup. That season we came through our qualifying group easily, scoring 29 goals and losing only 3 in six games. The opposition was all from the lower leagues but we easily disposed of Arbroath, Alloa and Dunfermline before going on to beat Partick Thistle in the two-legged quarter finals. This time we scored 7 goals in the two games and lost none. The semifinal brought us our first problem, but we beat Dundee United, the team who were eventually to pip us for the Premier League title by 1 point, by 3–2 over the two matches.

Then it was on to Hampden and a clash with our Old Firm rivals Rangers. Fifty-five thousand people saw the game in which Murdo MacLeod and I scored our goals. Jim Bett got one for Rangers and we ended up celebrating at Hampden!

I was happy to get that cup medal, but the one I wanted was the Scottish Cup and I was sure that this was the season when I would get it. Again, as in the League Cup, our form was impressive. We travelled to Kilbowie Park to play Clydebank in the first round proper and won 3–0. The next round we were at home to Dunfermline and repeated that result. We were in the quarter finals and hadn't lost a goal. Hearts came to Celtic Park next and, although we let them score, we won 4–1 and were poised for a Hampden semifinal against Aberdeen. The day before the game I twisted my ankle in training and couldn't play. Aberdeen scraped through 1–0 and went on to win the cup in extra time against Rangers with a goal by Eric Black. That was my Scottish Cup medal chance lost – the medal I probably wanted to win more than any other. I'll never get the chance again because I won't go back home to play. So it's a gap in my career that will never be filled.

10

Kenny, Danny and Pat – The Best of British

Any youngster who kicks a ball around the streets of Glasgow or London or Liverpool or Manchester or any city in the world will have heroes that they look up to. It's part of growing up; you look at one or two players and think that they have everything you admire in a footballer. Sometimes you are lucky enough to meet them, get their autographs, talk to them for a minute as they sign their name. Sometimes you are luckier still and get to know them as people. And if you are really lucky you may end up playing alongside them. That is what happened to me. I make no apologies for the fact that I hero-worshipped Kenny Dalglish when I was a kid at school in Glasgow and Kenny was playing for Celtic. There were other players too whom I admired when my old man took me to Celtic Park to see the games. But, always, there was something extra about Dalglish.

There were other good players in the team at that time, lots of good players, and a few others who were among the game's greats. Jimmy Johnstone was still there, still performing that right-wing magic that only he could turn on. I was lucky that my Dad had been going to watch Celtic all through the nine-championship-wins-in-a-row era. He knew all about the players and pointed things out to me. But with wee Jinky you didn't need to have anything poited out. He was God to everyone on the terraces, that wee man. I used to look at some of the tricks he did with the ball and say to myself, 'That's unbelievable!' Very few players are as gifted as Jinky was. I loved watching him. Everybody's a good judge on the terraces, but I was just a kid and took everything in uncritically. I was overwhelmed by the glamour of it all. There was no way that I was a good judge then, but I could recognize the extra-special talents of Jimmy Johnstone.

But there were other good players too. There was Harry Hood, big George Connelly, people like that, and I would watch what they were doing on the park. I would try the same moves when I was practising on my own, but there they were doing them in league games. It was hard to credit. People might think that I'm exaggerating about someone like Harry Hood. Perhaps Harry didn't do much at international level, but he was a good player for Celtic and scored a lot of goals. When I started going to the games there was a charisma about him. I always used to watch him, not just because he was a goal scorer but because he would try little tricks. For example, he would try to nutmeg opponents or beat them in a cheeky kind of way. It was the sort of thing that caught your eye and appealed to me, not just scoring goals, although that was impressive as well, but the cheeky, skilful aspects of the game. Even then I appreciated skilful play. Ever since I was really young it's been the skilful players who have impressed me most. I never paid much attention to the other side of the game. Workers didn't impress me to anything like the same extent. Nor did tacklers. OK, nowadays particularly, there are youngsters who try to follow the hard workers, admiring them more than some of the other players. That's fine because that's what they see to admire, but when I was young it never struck me as being the most important part of a player's make-up.

Even in defenders I admired skill rather than plain, hard tackling. In the short spell he had with Celtic I had tremendous admiration for Pat Stanton because he was always in control of defensive situations. He was one of the most skilful defenders I've ever seen. He read the game so well when he was playing as sweeper that he didn't have to make frantic last-gasp tackles. He seemed able to stroll around the penalty box clearing up. He had the ability to remain unruffled under pressure, and I used to look at him and wonder how he did it. Gradually I learned that Pat Stanton and players like him were able to look at any given situation developing in front of them and, through instinct or experience or a combination of both, be able to do exactly what was needed with the minimum of fuss.

Above all, though, there was Kenny Dalglish. It may sound a bit over the top when I try to explain how much he meant to me back then when I was just a youngster watching the games from the Parkhead terraces. People say that you can have visions about what you want to be or what you want to do in life. Well, for me, Kenny was that vision. Compared with other players he was on his own. I'd seen Jimmy Johnstone, watched all his tricks, marvelled with the thousands of others about how he did it all, and I knew that he was fantastic. But Dalglish was the best, the very best.

Kenny Dalglish had a bit of everything – some of the magic of wee Jimmy, some of the little touches of Harry Hood, some of the composure of Pat Stanton. From the beginning, from the first time I saw him, I knew that I was watching someone unique. No one else was like him, so far as I was concerned; no one else even approached him. Even at the warm-up, when he was shooting in before a game, I couldn't take my eyes off him. Even if I consciously tried to look away from him and watch another player my eyes kept going back to him. There was just something about him. I thought that if I could be a little bit like him as a player, then, if I decided to make football my career, I'd be a success. Of course, nothing else was considered as a career – I was setting my sights high!

Now that I know him, now I've met him, played alongside him and against him too, I find it hard to put into words what it was that set him apart from the other players. He is so natural, so utterly unaffected, and everything seems so easy for him. He is a naturally gifted player. Some people will reckon that he's lucky to be blessed with the gift he has – but when you are blessed that way you still have to work hard. He has an amazing talent; you can't help but admire his skill. He has absolutely everything. Talent on the park and a perfect temperament off it. He is a one-off. You just have to hold your hands up and say, 'He's the King.' I call him that, King – and I mean it.

He has been tremendous to me. When I first moved down to Arsenal and had a few problems he would phone me for a little chat, and if I needed advice I could call him. Yet even when I speak to him like that I find it hard to let the reality sink in. It's fine when we're talking to each other; I can crack a joke and have a laugh with him. But when I put the phone down I have to pinch myself to prove that it's really happening. I feel like telling the whole world, 'That was Kenny Dalglish on the phone – my mate.' That's an international player talking – but the kid who first watched Kenny play isn't too far away at times! He remains the best player I've ever seen.

Now, of course, he has taken another step in his career by becoming manager of Liverpool. And he's still playing for them too. I don't know anyone else in the game who could take on the double role that Kenny has taken on and, as I'm writing this, make a success of both! Kenny grew up under Jock Stein and Bob Paisley and he will have learned from them. But he also has presence, that little something that brings respect. He was always respected as a player. No matter the company he was in, people had respect for Kenny Dalglish. That is bound to spill over into his new career. He will be successful, even though it is hard to adjust quickly to moving from the playing side to the management side. With Kenny, of course, it is even harder because he has a foot in both camps – as a player and as boss. A lot of people said he wouldn't be able to handle it, but he has managed to look after both jobs. He is about the only guy I know who could take everything in his stride the way he seems to have done so far. It's just another facet of the man.

It's been amazing how he has left himself out of the team when he felt that that was the right decision for Liverpool. When players with his reputation drop out of a side there are usually screaming headlines about it in the newspapers. Kenny has been able to do it without having it noised all over the place. He has made the decision and announced it without any fuss. Even when he was aiming for his hundredth cap for Scotland he risked missing it by dropping himself from the Liverpool league side. The man is so honest, he will never make a selfish choice and put himself or his own ambitions above those of Liverpool. Who else would do that kind of thing?

Yet, for me, he is still a great player and Liverpool miss him when he is not on the team. When we beat them at Highbury he wasn't playing and his absence was felt. There are other good players in the team, marvellous players in fact, but he has a subtlety about his play that others can't match.

That's on the field; off the field he can be less subtle, much more direct. If he wants to make a point about something that happened in a match then he will tell you straight out. And he will tell you in what might seem to be a hurtful way. But although you may feel hurt at the time, if you stop to think about what he's said, you realize that Kenny is trying to help you. He is telling it to you straight because he feels it will be of benefit to you in your career. He'll never shirk telling a player that he's made a mistake or let the team down or cost them a game. He'll spell it out with complete honesty even if that means upsetting someone. He may have a nasty streak, as he says himself, but it's the man's way. He has a special kind of integrity which no one will ever be able to take away from him. As a manager he's the kind of person that you can take your troubles

105

to if necessary. You know where you stand with him. He'll never duck out on any situation.

Naturally Liverpool haven't made Kenny manager without a great deal of thought. For instance, Kenny has Bob Paisley at his elbow and if he's in doubt about anything then Bob can help him. There are certain to be situations that Kenny will face as a manager which he never knew as a player – Bob can nudge him in the right direction. Moving out of a dressing room where you have mates and becoming their boss can present particular problems. Terry Neill suffered because one or two players at Highbury had played alongside him at club or national level, and that led to too much familiarity. You have to guard against it, but Kenny will be able to handle the situation. He has grown up in the Liverpool tradition and he'll keep that alive. Football is supposed to have changed a lot – I don't know if Liverpool have changed all that much over the past ten years, or if they will change much in the next ten either. They keep the game simple; they try to play football all the time and they are marvellously organized. Kenny will keep that going. Without any doubt, they are the best club side I have ever come up against ... and, remember, I turned them down!

Anyhow, back to the King, and remember my prediction. I think he will be as good a manager as he has been a player, and he is the best player I've ever seen or been involved with. There are still a few months to go to the World Cup finals in Mexico but I'm betting on Kenny getting there with Scotland. If he does he will crown an incredible record. After a long spell during which Scotland didn't reach the World Cup finals – from 1938 until 1974 – the international side has qualified *four* times in succession. Kenny has helped them into the finals every time. He played in West Germany, in Argentina and in Spain. If he gets to Mexico he will be the first British player to take part in four finals and will join a very elite band of players; perhaps only Pele and Dino Zoff have equalled that. I'm backing Kenny to join them. As well as his extraordinary ability Kenny has a resilience which has carried him through all these campaigns. People say he has had bad World Cups, but the team has never done well in the finals and because of that he has suffered in the minds of some. He gets the blame because of who he is, yet back he comes. He was almost written off after Spain when he was dropped from the team during the opening group matches. A few months later he was back in the side, and he is still there. Remember the ball he sent through for Frank McAvennie to score against Australia at Hampden? Remember the goal he scored against Spain? Both incidents were vintage Dalglish.

There must have been something special in the air around Celtic Park in 1967. That was the year the team won the European Cup, the first British team ever to do so, and two youngsters joined up as reserve players. One was Kenny Dalglish; the other was Danny McGrain, a player who has had more influence on my career than anyone else I've ever lined up with. While Kenny was my inspiration, Danny was my guide when I went to Celtic Park as a teenager. I call him 'Shep' because he's just like an old shepherd, looking after all the younger players, giving them advice, trying to keep them on the right road, and still one of the best full backs in Scotland. Danny is an example to everyone who has ever come into contact with him. Like Kenny, he is the complete professional. There is something great about these guys. Danny used to pick me up every morning to take me to training. He'd pick me up when I was an apprentice and when I got into the first team until I could drive myself. When I broke my leg it was Danny, again, who would stop at the house, come in, get me into the back of the car and take me to the Park for treatment.

I consider myself lucky to have come under Danny's influence. He took me under his wing. He would talk a lot about the game, and I learned a great deal listening to him. Danny and Kenny were great players, two of the greatest Celtic and Scotland players ever, but at the

start they had to live in the shadow of the Lisbon Lions.
They grew up with that team's reputation hanging over
them. But they had played with the lads who had won
the European Cup, beating Inter Milan in the final, and
they learned from them. Danny used to tell me about
what he'd learned from some of the players who had
gone ahead of him. In his turn he passed his knowledge
on to me and other young players. He was vitally
important in teaching me how the game should be
played.

At his best Danny was the finest right back I've ever
known. He could come upfield and attack like a forward
and he could stay back and defend with the best of them.
One of the biggest compliments I can pay Danny is to
say that the nearest thing I've ever seen to him is my
Arsenal team-mate Kenny Sansom. Kenny's a left back,
but he is the kind of complete player that Danny was.
Even now, towards the end of his career, I still rate
Danny very highly. I have always felt that he could
have played in the international team a little longer. He
decided in Spain that it was time to give up his Scotland
place, but since then he has stayed in the Celtic side
and played for them against some of the top teams in
Europe. I'm not criticizing lads like Stevie Nicol and
Richard Gough, who have come into the Scotland side
at right back, but Danny could have won a few more
caps. Perhaps he felt that he had had enough of the
game at that level. He had had his innings, but despite
getting older he can still make the game look easy, he
reads it so well and uses the ball so naturally. Everyone
at Celtic Park admires him. All of us used to look up to
him, and he deserved that kind of respect. When I left
Celtic Danny was in his thirties yet he was still training
as hard as ever and still working at the game. People
like Danny McGrain are worth their weight in gold to
any club. What an example he provides for every player
at Celtic Park!

I'll never forget all the things he did for me. When I
broke my leg I was very worried about it. You tell

yourself not to worry when the doctors say, 'Yes, you'll be fine in four months,' but four months is a long time when you're a youngster trying to get back into the first team. When I was feeling depressed Danny talked me out of it. He kept encouraging me, lifting me, reassuring me. That is the kind of man he is. He is a professional who cares about his fellow professionals. I still find it hard to believe that Kenny and Danny emerged from the same year's intake of players at Celtic.

The other player I have the same sort of feeling for is Pat Jennings, who was still with Arsenal when I joined the club. Big Pat is another of that same breed. I used to call him 'God' because he seemed to know everything about the game. If you needed advice or help Pat was there. I think that every club needs that kind of figure. I've been lucky to have my education looked after by so many good players. Kenny was undoubtedly the inspiration, Danny was the player who was the major influence, and Big Pat — well, he helped provide the finishing touches!

My hope is that I have picked up enough from them down through the years to make as big a success of my career as they made of theirs. There may have been a couple of bad years, a couple of years when I was trying to find my way. I hope the bad times are over; if they are and if things go right it will be because of the principles that I learned from Danny and Kenny in particular. The kind of schooling you get from people like them can't be bought. I doubt if it can even be duplicated anywhere else.

11

My Scotland Return

The testimonial match for John McMaster which was
played at Pittodrie just before Christmas in 1985 proved
an important milestone in my career. For a start, it came
at just the right time for me. I was beginning to score
goals for Arsenal and people were talking about me for
the Scotland squad again. In the testimonial I was
playing alongside international players and Alex
Ferguson had a chance to see me in action.

A month later I was picked for the Scotland side
which was to play against Israel in Tel Aviv! The Scotland boss, Alex Ferguson, had liked what he'd seen of
me in the testimonial match, he knew that I was scoring
goals with Arsenal and picked me for the squad. Then
he came down to watch me play at Villa Park in the
Milk Cup quarter final against Aston Villa. I scored
again that night, and I think that's when he decided
that he would play me against the Israelis.

Mind you, there was still a problem before I was
allowed to join the squad which was to fly out from
Glasgow on the Sunday before the game. On the
preceding Saturday we drew 1–1 with Villa and the
Football League ordered a replay the following week at
the same time as we were supposed to be playing Israel
and England was playing Egypt. I had a few hours
of worry until the whole matter was sorted out, but
fortunately the league officials changed their minds and
the players on international duty were allowed to go
abroad. It seemed strange for the league to take that
attitude in a World Cup season; if England had not been

playing then I would probably have had to stay at home. But a plea from the England boss Bobby Robson brought about a change of heart, and the chance I had been praying for was on.

Being recalled to the Scotland side was one of the most important things in my life. Whenever the World Cup competition comes around it is on everyone's minds. Mexico was no different. It loomed at the end of the season, dwarfing everything else. The finals of the World Cup are the most important games in the career of those footballers lucky enough to play in them. Whole generations of great players in Scotland had missed the chance of playing on the most massive stage of all. And it was the same for other marvellous players with Northern Ireland, and England, and Wales. Think of George Best, Jim Baxter, Billy McNeill, Kevin Keegan, who was limited to one very brief appearance in Spain, and Ian Rush and Mark Hughes, who have missed out on Mexico as Wales failed to qualify again.

In Scotland, the World Cup has dominated international thinking for the last dozen years. Before then the national side failed to qualify in three successive World Cup competitions. They didn't play in Chile in 1962, although they were desperately unlucky to lose in a qualifying play-off against Czechoslovakia, the team that went on to reach the final. In 1966 Scotland went out when Italy won the qualifying section and so they didn't make the short trip south of the Border to play in the finals in England. Four years later, when the finals were in Mexico for the first time, they lost to West Germany, who took third place on that occasion.

Everything changed in 1974. This time Scotland were the only British team to go to West Germany. They repeated the feat four years later when, once again, they were Britain's sole representatives, this time in Argentina. They followed that up by qualifying for Spain in 1982 and for Mexico in 1986 – a marvellous record for a country our size.

Curiously, the European championship has not

111

caught the imagination of the fans to anything like the same extent. The World Cup eclipses everything else. For people of my age it's almost unthinkable for Scotland not to qualify because we have been able to see them play in three finals in recent years, whereas before that time the World Cup seemed a million miles away from us.

I suppose that's why I was so anxious to push myself back into contention. Obviously the glamour of the tournament appeals to me, but now it is so much a part of the lore of the Scottish game that I want to taste it for myself. I listen to Dalglish and McGrain and Souness and all the others talking about different matches – ones that I have watched on the telly – and I want to be a part of all that. At the start of the 1985–86 season, after two disappointing years with Arsenal, I would sustain myself with the prospect of Mexico. That, and the thought of achieving success at club level, because the one could lead to the other – there were two dreams to be realized. First of all, I thought, I must try to get things right with Arsenal. If that happens and if the club can get a good run of results, then the Scotland chance could come up. That's the way I worked it out and luckily that's the way it happened. From the moment in November when I was moved up front permanently, everything seemed to change.

When the draw was made for the World Cup finals my ambitions were intensified even further. Sometimes you may be drawn in a poor group, not necessarily poor in terms of ability but poor in terms of appeal. This time, however, we were in the top group in the whole of the Mexican finals. When the draw was announced there we were with West Germany, twice winners of the trophy and always powerful in any World Cup competition; Uruguay, also twice winners of the cup, and Denmark, in the finals for the first time, but boasting one of the most exciting sides in Europe. The Danes, not seeded because of their previously poor World Cup record, were the side every team wanted to avoid.

For me, though, the other members of the group made the prospect of playing for my country even more exciting and challenging. After all, if you are going to take part in the greatest soccer show on earth then you will be comparing yourself with the best the rest of the world can offer. To lose in the highest company is no disgrace. My other thought was that on the previous occasions when Scotland had failed in the World Cup finals they had failed because of the poor results against the supposedly weaker teams in the group. In West Germany against Zaïre the Scots won 2–0 and struggled in the second half. Another goal or two would have taken us into the second phase. Against Iran in Argentina we could only draw 1–1, while both Peru and Holland, the two teams who qualified from the group, each beat the Iranians by 3 goals. In Spain we allowed New Zealand to score 2 goals against us and although we won the game 5–2 we went out on goal difference for the third time in succession. Yet on each occasion we were able to raise our game against the quality teams in the groups we were drawn in. In Germany we drew with Brazil and Yugoslavia; in Argentina we beat Holland, who went on to reach the final; and in Spain we drew with Russia, who had been strongly tipped to do well in the tournament.

The prospect of meeting the top-quality sides in the toughest group didn't frighten me off. It made me even more determined to get to Mexico if I could. That's why being recalled to the side for Israel was so important. It was possibly the most important thing that had happened to me since I first started playing the game. Getting into the first team at Celtic was important, getting my first cap was important, establishing myself with Arsenal was important, but this topped everything.

It had been difficult to get back into the squad; hence the importance of what most people would regard as a simple friendly in Tel Aviv. Scotland only had three games or so to play before making the journey to Mexico when I was brought back. Time had been running out for me. But I had the example of my pal Frank McAvennie at West Ham, who had forced his way into the side a month or two earlier. Frank had been scoring well since joining West Ham and was called up for a friendly against East Germany. He then played in the two final qualifying ties against Australia at Hampden and in Melbourne's Olympic Stadium. Before that he had not had a mention, but after those games it looked as if he had booked his Mexico spot. But not to be in the side with only three or four games before Mexico was leaving it too late. I had to make the most of my chance in Israel, and so the importance of that match was emphasized in my own mind.

I found it great to be back, simply to be a part of things again: seeing some of the old faces, working with Alex Ferguson in training, sharing a room with my old Celtic buddy Roy Aitken, and simply knowing that I was involved with the international squad. A few faces were missing – the Liverpool lads Stevie Nicol, Alan Hansen and Kenny weren't there, and Graeme Souness was missing because Sampdoria had an Italian Cup tie to play. But lots of the other lads were there and after a few hours in their company I realized how much I had missed being with them all. There's a great spirit about this Scotland squad. It was there when the World Cup campaign began and it was even stronger now that the lads had qualified and the countdown to Mexico had started.

Apart from that, there was the memory of being left behind at Highbury when various international games were on. I used to get so fed up. Highbury was like a ghost ground when international matches were being played and players were away with England or Ireland. As I hadn't been picked for Scotland, I had to train with five or six other players who had also been left behind. It seemed like the worst time of my life, so not to have to spend another lonely week at the training ground was a bonus for me! Just being back made me feel better, and to be playing again was a great boost. Perhaps the game against Israel wasn't too bright for various reasons and perhaps the fans back home were bored stiff watching the first half on the box, but it was vital for me to be there and to play, even though it was scarcely the most enjoyable game I've played in.

The fact that I was playing for Scotland, that I was a member of my country's World Cup squad again, made me happy, but the pitch was probably the worst playing surface I've ever seen at senior level. It was diabolical. Also there was no real atmosphere. The game was being shown live on television so only four or five thousand people turned up in the Ramat Gan Stadium. Because of the small crowd it didn't seem like an international. That spoilt things a bit. It made it seem insignificant and yet we were trying to work out a new approach which we might use in Mexico. Alex Ferguson wants to play possession football there and this was an opportunity to try it out. When you are building towards a World Cup competition every game is important; and despite the atmosphere the Israel game was important because I really wanted to do well.

The night before the game the boss had stressed to us that one of the biggest boosts we could have before going to Mexico – no matter which of us actually goes in the end – would be to have a long undefeated run behind us. We had a run of six games; the World Cup defeat by Wales at Hampden had been the last time the team had lost. He is right, too; I don't think a team can go into any tournament better prepared than that. We won the game in Israel, despite the fact it was away from home. No international match is easy to win away from home these days. It doesn't matter where you go in the world, it can be difficult to get the result you want. The smaller countries are organizing themselves so much better, making it harder for their opponents, and Israel made it hard for us for a lot of the game.

I teamed up with Graeme Sharp of Everton and our partnership came close to working out well. The worry was that neither Graeme nor I scored; it took a goal

115

from Paul McStay, the Celtic midfield player, to give us the result. The main strikers haven't been scoring consistently and the boss has tried various permutations. It was good with Sharpie because at Arsenal I'd been playing with a big lad, Niall Quinn, and so I was quite used to the role I was asked to play. But I felt rather sorry for Graeme. It's never as easy for front players when your team is playing a containing game as we were doing. The others weren't getting the ball up to us as early as they do at club level, but that's something that will come with time. Quite a few of our players were together for the first time and so that created its own problems. There were also two Israeli defenders who went everywhere with us. They played man for man at the back, with the former Liverpool defender Avi Cohen playing as a sweeper behind the markers.

However, I certainly felt by the end of the game that Graeme Sharp and I could work together. OK, their men went tight on us, but there were a couple of times when we escaped them. They were also a bit tasty; they didn't mind having a whack at you from behind when you were going to pick up the ball. The guy who was going with Sharpie hit him a few dull ones, and the man marking me wasn't too short on the physical side of the game either. But you have to learn to live with that. Most important, even though the trip was short – we had only one training session together before playing – there were some good things which came out of the match.

We won and so kept up our unbeaten run. We tried to play the kind of game that the manager wanted and, given that the ground would have upset any passing movements, we managed to do that in the second half. And there was one chance when I might have scored, a shot from the edge of the box which hit the face of the crossbar. I wish that one had gone in. It would have demoralized the Israelis even more and we might have won by several goals. It would have also given me a scoring comeback, which was what I wanted.

116

I was under no illusions when I joined the squad that it was going to be easy to book a Mexico ticket. Alex Ferguson made it clear that I couldn't be judged on only one game, and earlier he had said that my skills would benefit the team in the World Cup finals. But on looking around at the other contenders I reckoned that Scotland have the best strike force they've ever had. In England there's Kenny Dalglish, who is, well, just Kenny, which means extra special; then you have Frank McAvennie at West Ham, Dave Speedie at Chelsea, Graeme Sharp at Everton, and me. If things keep going well for the four of us we'll be sharing a hundred goals between us by the end of the season. Then in Scotland there are Mo Johnston of Celtic and Paul Sturrock of Dundee United; and on the Continent Steve Archibald with Barcelona. That's a fairly formidable list of names for any manager to ponder over and it's obvious that there is not room for all of them in the Scotland squad. That's why I see it as a battle royal for the available places over the next few seasons.

Personally I believe that I can do a job for the side. The manager has stressed to the lads that he wants them to play as they do for their clubs. He wants us to play according to our strengths and if the other players give us the chances then perhaps the goal famine that has afflicted Scotland strikers will disappear.

One of the problems which may have contributed to the lack of goals has been the number of enforced changes that have been made in the side. For one reason or another players haven't had long runs together. I had a short initial spell with the team, then I went out, and because I wasn't scoring regularly with my club and was being changed from position to position there I didn't get back for a while. Then little Mo Johnston had a short run in the side, and then Graeme Sharp came in, then Frank McAvennie and Dave Speedie. For the Israel game, Frank and Dave Speedie were involved in games with their clubs and couldn't make the trip, while Mo hadn't been scoring at Parkhead and was left out. It's

117

difficult to build up an understanding until you have played together a few times. I said before that little things worked out with Sharpie and me. In earlier games I felt that I had a fair understanding with Kenny – but it's easy to play alongside Kenny because he is the player whom the opposition are always wanting to mark. He's the one who gets all the attention and so you sometimes get an opportunity to sneak into gaps he has created just by being on the field. In the early days I also had an understanding with Graeme Souness. After one or two games I began to know instinctively how he was going to play the ball forward. That kind of relationship does develop at international level, but it takes time. The changes which have been forced on Scotland for different reasons over the past year or so have made it harder for understandings to develop, but if the manager continues with his instructions to players to play as they would for their clubs then that could change. I've felt better since going up front with Arsenal, and that's where the boss had me playing in Tel Aviv. I'm sure that if the ball is played to me the way I like it – to my feet around the penalty box – then I'll be able to do a good job for my country. I'm desperate to prove myself again. Sometimes I look at Kenny Dalglish and study his record, and it comes home to me how much there is left to achieve in the game. If I make him my target and achieve half the amount of success he has with his clubs and with Scotland then I won't go very far wrong.

It was easier for me to return to the side in the game against Israel than it had been at the start of the World Cup qualifying games. I had been asked to go on as substitute and felt very much on the fringe of the game. I came on and scored in a couple of matches, but found it much harder than in the Israel game. It is probably a matter of confidence. In the qualifiers I was getting ten minutes here and ten minutes there and that was difficult to cope with. When you come on you're so anxious to do something in the ten minutes left of the game, you often miss because you are trying too hard.

Part of the problem was the fact that my confidence was rather low because I wasn't doing well at Arsenal. I was having a bit of a rough time with the club and, as anyone will tell you, a striker thrives on success. When it came to the game in Israel I was full of confidence because of the goals I had been getting for Arsenal. Scoring there so regularly and grabbing a hat-trick at Grimsby had given me a tremendous lift. When I left Glasgow to go on the trip I felt that I deserved to be there with the rest of the lads, that I had earned the right to be with them, if you like, and that I was playing well enough to get into the team. That's how it worked out in the end. My state of mind was right by that time. Your psychological outlook is very important when you are are playing at the top level.

There is nothing higher than the finals of the World Cup. If you're a tennis player you have Wimbledon as the biggest stage; a golfer has the Open or the Masters; but this is bigger than any of them. Players have the chance to become world-wide celebrities. Winning a cup or playing at Wembley or Hampden is a big event in your own country – it may even spread your reputation to Europe – but the World Cup takes you everywhere that football is played. That's why it has mattered so much for me to get to the finals.

I love the big stage; I love testing myself against the best players, and in the World Cup I can do that. There's nothing more I can ask for from football than to be able to play in the World Cup finals. If I get to Mexico then I'm sure I'll finish up hungry for more – because that's how Kenny Dalglish and Graeme Souness have been. They come back from one World Cup and start talking about the next one – that's the effect it has on great players. I want to join them.

12

Happiness at Highbury

When it took me so long to settle down at Arsenal there were so many rumours flying around about my future that even I began to wonder what was going to happen to me! There were stories that Don Howe was going to sell me because I didn't fit into his plans; suggestions that my old boss at Celtic, Billy McNeill, was to take me back and buy me for Manchester City, that I was ready to leave London and head for the Continent. The rumour factory worked overtime and not one of the stories had any truth at all.

My contract at Arsenal was for four years and that means I must consider my future in the summer of 1987, and not before, although I am ready to commit myself to another long-term contract with Arsenal if one is offered me. In a way I feel I owe that to the club because they were so patient while I was going through those difficult times in settling down. And I certainly owe it to the supporters. These people have been marvellous, especially the lads who stand on the North Bank. They have believed in me from the first moment that I joined the club. When I wasn't playing well they stuck by me, supporting me, making me feel a lot better, and it is thanks to them that I was able to keep going when things looked pretty bleak.

Arsenal, of course, as I pointed out before, are one of the world's *great* clubs. No matter where you go, people know about the Arsenal. When I was in Israel with Scotland I was constantly surrounded with autograph hunters, all of them Arsenal fans. It's the same no matter which country you are in, and I don't honestly see myself being able to play for any other British club. Circumstances can always change, but no other team has the kind of aura that there is at Highbury. To move to any other team is to take a step backwards.

Then there is the question of going abroad. I had various offers when I was leaving Celtic, offers which would have taken me to Italy and made me very wealthy. I know now that I did the right thing in turning them down; although the challenge would have been exciting it would have been no greater than the challenge we have had at Arsenal. Added to that, I like London. I like the people and I like the place and after a couple of years of problems I was able to settle in a pleasant area, make good solid friendships and sort out my off-field life.

For the last item I have to thank Jerome Anderson. I suppose most folk would describe Jerome as my agent because he now looks after my business interests. Before Jerome came along a couple of agents gave me headaches. Yet he's more than an agent, he's a mate, a good friend who is also an Arsenal supporter and who has given me nothing but good advice since we got together. It isn't easy to find the right kind of person to take care of business affairs for you. Sometimes they try to do too much or, rather, they try to get you to do too much and your form on the field suffers. I know that. I called a halt to a lot of the activities I was involved in and now I simply follow Jerome's advice. If he recommends a deal which is advantageous to me, and which won't hurt my image or upset anyone at Arsenal, I know I can trust his judgement.

People outside the game sometimes say that players don't need agents. But we do need them because, like anyone else, we have to try to make provision for our future. The game can bring you good rewards but your playing career doesn't last a lifetime; when you're young it is too easy to forget that, to live for the day and forget about what tomorrow will bring. You need someone with good business sense to help guide and advise you. Jerome has done that for me and he has done it very well. The club approve, too, of the way he has handled me. The Champagne Charlie image is *out* – it was never true in any case, but I was pushed into certain situations which made the public believe that image was me. Now I'm never exposed to that kind of publicity. Jerome makes sure of that, and I appreciate all the help he has given me. His influence off the field has helped me to settle in better in my third season, but on the field there were other reasons too. On the personal side I had a goal-scoring run, and the club had a little run of good results as well.

When I look back at the first two seasons it isn't hard to understand why things were tough for me. The team wasn't doing particularly well and I was trying to find my way in a new type of league. At the end of the day I believe that I'm a better player, but at first the systems used in the First Division were alien to me and to what I believed in. Even now, although I accept the need for organization, I still prefer the entertainers of the game. I grew up worshipping people like Rodney Marsh, Stan Bowles and Bertie Auld. I was fed stories of Charlie Tully and Jim Baxter, players the fans loved. It's the way I wanted to play the game. That is why, even now, I prefer to watch Glenn Hoddle than Bryan Robson. I'm not knocking Bryan when I say that. It's just that Hoddle has the kind of skills that I have always admired. But players like that seem to inspire some kind of mistrust among coaches and managers in England.

Possibly I suffered a little from that. As a team Celtic never had the tactical awareness that is demanded in the English First Division. Their fans were reared on a diet of attacking football and that's what they want to see. That was the case when I was there, and I doubt very much if it has changed since. So when I came to England I didn't possess the defensive qualities that even forwards require – I doubt if I possessed any at all! It was part of the game that I had to brush up on.

It will never be my strong point, and I was never happier than when Don Howe finally told me to go upfield and stay there. That's the place where I know how to play best. I wasn't taught the game – I learned it in the Glasgow streets. I can remember being with the Scotland Youth team once, and Walter Smith, the Dundee United coach who is now Alex Ferguson's right-hand man with Scotland, said to me, 'Look, there is nothing in the way of natural skills that I can teach you. All I can do is help you add little bits here and there.' He did too – he taught me a couple of things which I have never forgotten and which have been useful; additions to my own natural game. But what he was really telling me was that he didn't want to start changing my natural game. He didn't want to tinker too much with the things I was good at. Probably he realized that it was the only way I knew how to play the game. I don't want to see a side which is full of hard-working runners and nothing else. You need other players with style and with flair, and players like that shouldn't be curbed too much.

It makes me wince when I read about the school of excellence set up by the Football Association and how they have brought someone over from Holland to teach kids how to dribble the ball. Dribbling is something that comes naturally. My worry over the school of excellence is that it might produce players who all do the same thing, football robots who won't be able to think for themselves or enjoy themselves when they play. Playing as well as watching should be enjoyable. If I didn't enjoy the game I'd be worried. It shouldn't be dull and repetitive; it should be exciting all the time. Above all, it should be the beautiful game that Pele loved so much.

Deep down in my heart of hearts, I fear that won't be possible any more. If you go out to entertain but cannot win, then crowd numbers fall, managers are sacked and players are axed. That's the way life is these days. It would be nice, though, to be able to turn back the clock to the days when the entertainers were allowed to express themselves and when success was not all important.

However, I have to admit to having mixed feelings. The lack of success at Arsenal in my first two years depressed me deeply – and it takes a lot to get me down. We lost FA Cup ties at places like Middlesbrough and York and were knocked out of the Milk Cup at Walsall. I thought then, and even now I look back and think the same, this is not what I came to England for! I came looking for the glamour, for the kind of success I'd had with Celtic, for the games in the major European tournaments which can help make any team's season. None of that was happening. Then, in the third season, came the better signs, and with those signs came my improvement in form. We went to Grimsby, and with so many of the TV and newspaper experts expecting us to lose we won easily and I scored my first hat-trick for the club. That may yet prove to be one of the turning points for the club and for my career at Highbury. New players have come in and all of us seem to be pulling in the same direction at last.

Stewart Robson broke through into the England team and afterwards said that his understanding with me had helped him get there. That was nice of Stewart – and I must say he has helped me too. There is an almost telepathic understanding between us. I seem to know when he will break forward, when he will release the ball and when he will look for a return pass. It's good and it feels comfortable. Big Niall Quinn has done magnificently too. Maybe he's still a little soft, a bit too nice for such a big fellow, but he can play and is keen to do well.

As I write, happy days are here again at Highbury. Maybe some day soon I'll be able to tell Kenny Dalglish and Graeme Souness and everyone else that I did make the right decision when I was transferred by Celtic. That's what I'm hoping for!